CHRIS HOWKINS
NEW TOWPATH BOOK

WRITTEN AND ILLUSTRATED
    by Chris Howkins.
    © Chris Howkins 1990

FIRST PUBLISHED 1983
    REPRINTED WITH AMENDMENTS 1986
    ISBN 0 9509105 0 3
THIS NEW EDITION, REWRITTEN AND ILLUSTRATED
    1990   ISBN 0 9509105 5 4
    REPRINTED 1992
PUBLISHED
    by Chris Howkins,
    70, Grange Road,
    New Haw,
    Weybridge,
    Surrey.
    KT15 3RH

PRINTED IN ENGLAND
    by Unwin Brothers Ltd.,
    The Gresham Press,
    Old Woking,
    Surrey.
    GU22 9LH

Guildford

CONTENTS

RIVER : Natural Waterway

CANAL : Man-made Waterway

NAVIGATION : River made Navigable

River Thames

Thames Lock   WEYBRIDGE

Weybridge Lock

Coxes Lock   ADDLESTONE

New Haw Lock

Pyrford Lock

Walsham Gates   RIPLEY

Newark Lock

Paper Court Lock   OLD WOKING

Worsfold Gates   SEND

Triggs Lock

Bowers Lock

Stoke Lock

Mill Mead Lock   GUILDFORD

St. Catherine's Lock

Unstead Lock

Catteshall Lock

Godalming Wharf

Wey Navigation

Godalming Navigation

River Wey

INTRODUCTION

Imagine some water meadows under a dark winter sky about to storm, with a low sun lighting the oaks in greenish gold and the birch trees in reddish purple, all contrasting sharply with the winter emerald of the grass. The air is rich with the scent of winter. The lapwing calls are shredding in the wind.

Not all of that can be drawn; some things are for the heart only. What this book does contain is a selection of notes, sketches and drawings relating to what can be seen when walking the towpath of the Wey and Godalming Navigations in Surrey. For nearly twenty miles this stretches through historic and often beautiful landscapes. There's more than enough for these ninety six pages! It's been very difficult to decide what to include and what to omit, but if this final selection enhances people's appreciation just a little it will have served well.

THE NEW EDITION

The first version of the Towpath Book was published in 1983. By 1986 when it needed reprinting only a little updating was needed. By 1989, when a further reprint was needed, over a third of the pages needed changing and there was so much more that could be added.

Consequently it was decided to re-write the whole book but in the style of the first, which proved so popular.

The text now concentrates much more on the waterway itself to reflect increasing interest in local history. It incorporates answers to the most frequent questions asked at the end of talks and in particular says which sections are canal and which are river, which are old and which date only from the 1930s. Nevertheless, this is only a guide, not the full story.

The illustrations have been re-selected to add over seventy not in the first version, such as the aerial views and those of the Dapdune Heritage Centre. Some bird illustrations have been taken from "Enjoying Wisley's Birds" while other material has been re-issued from the Doorstep Book which has been out of print for some years but which is still in demand. The Doorstep Book will not be re-issued; there have been too many changes. Along the towpath there have been changes too but happily some are for the better.

THE NAVIGATIONS
AND
THE NATIONAL TRUST

The National Trust received on behalf of the nation the Wey Navigation as a donation from its last owner, Mr. H.W. Stevens, in 1964.

The Commissioners of the Godalming Navigation transferred their length to Guildford Corporation in 1968 and they in turn transferred it to the National Trust.

It's not the easiest of properties for the National Trust to maintain and preserve. It is only about 50 yards wide but 20 miles long. That gives 40 miles of boundary with 1000 neighbours living in 4 different Boroughs.

Then there are all the problems with the water itself — avoiding pollution, flood control etc. There are 16 locks, 12 weirs, 50 weir structures, 24 bridges, 13 cottages and 24 other buildings plus their own 'fleet' of 11 craft.

To cope with all this there are only 8 full time and 7 part time staff, on a fine budget too. The property has to raise its own funds; no money comes from the Government. Consequently volunteers are highly valued. Some thirty give regularly their time and professional services - as surveyors, solicitors, valuers, wardens etc. The overall Manager is Mr. R.J. Nicholls MBE BEM MISM

25ᵀᴴ ANNIVERSARY

In September 1989 the National Trust celebrated their 25 years of ownership aboard the horse drawn narrowboat "Iona" on a four day run down the full length of the Navigations.

It caught the romantic imagination for days long gone. It also showed how much hard work was involved — and that was without a full load, rising floods and high winds which had so often been the lot of the bargees.

NAVIGATION OFFICE

The National Trust Navigation Office:

Dapdune Lea,
Wharf Road,
Guildford,
Surrey,
GU1 4RR

Telephone Guildford 0483
61389

SIR RICHARD WESTON

AND THE FOUNDING OF THE

WEY NAVIGATION

A3

Wey

The creative force behind the scheme to make the Wey navigable was Sir Richard Weston of Sutton Place, Guildford. In his day the estates were far more extensive than today and the River Wey cut through them.

The Sutton (southern) estates had been part of the royal manor of Woking and were granted to one of Richard's ancestors by Henry VIII in 1521 for loyal service. The present house, where Richard was born in 1591, was built 1523-5, by an earlier Richard who died in 1542. It was the first or second great English house to be built in the new style without fortifications. At about the same time Henry VIII's building programme at adjoining Woking was about the last in the old fortified style.

England was enjoying the stable régime of the Tudors and so, as a restless teenager, Richard Weston was able to travel abroad and did so, with an eye alert for fresh ideas about making land profitable. Soon after his return his father died, in 1613, and Richard took up his title, his inheritance and a will to implement his new ideas.

Sir Richard's main concern was not to improve transport by water but the productivity of his lands. Agriculture was limited much more by the weather than is the case today. Only a small breeding stock of cattle could be kept alive through the winter on whatever hay had been harvested successfully the summer before. That was often running short by early spring. If cold March winds and sharp frosts delayed the new season's grass it could be a disaster year. There

6

was a series of bad harvests in the 1590s followed by more
in 1608, 1613, 1617 and 1622. By this time Sir Richard was
at work trying to improve his chances. He introduced an
idea he'd seen in the Low Countries. There they dropped
boards across the drainage channels to deliberately
flood the pastures with running water for a couple of
days. That both irrigated them against the drying
winds and raised the temperature a couple of
degrees to ward off frosts. So Sir Richard cut a channel
past the meanders in the river through his estates and
installed Surrey's first pound lock to control the waters,
at Stoke, in about 1618. That enabled him to 'float' his pastures.
    He'd seen the channels in the Low Countries being used as
highways and he didn't fail to realise that traffic on the Wey
might like to take a short cut through his channel and, of
course, pay him a toll for the privilege. Thus began a life-long
struggle to canalise the whole river, from Guildford down to
the Thames and so to London docks and world trade.

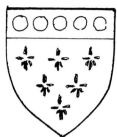

Sir Richard Weston's arms

Trying to sell that idea to landowners was very difficult. What Sir Richard needed was royal backing and that's what the king gave in 1635. Alas, the king was Charles I and his downfall meant any royalist sympathies were dangerous. Worse, the Protestant Puritans came to power and Sir Richard was a Roman Catholic recusant.

The puritans reduced Sir Richard's wealth and power, forcing him to sell off lands at Clandon and Merrow to Sir Richard Onslow to become Clandon Park. This may have been a diplomatic move as Onslow was an important Parliamentarian. Next year the Civil War began and Weston was forced into exile in Europe.

Another Parliamentarian comes to the rescue - Major James Pitson, Commissioner for Surrey, who arbitrated successfully for Weston's pardon and the return of his estates.

In 1650 the scheme moved forward when the bill for its construction was presented to Parliament on December 26th. That was not Boxing Day as the Puritans had banned the celebration of Christmas. Six months later the Act was passed, on June 26th 1651. Sir Richard had overcome his Royalist and Catholic problems by keeping his name out of these final approaches. Instead, the application was made in the name of the townsmen of Guildford, Sir Richard having persuaded them that an improved transport system would help revive their declining trade.

Construction work began on making 15½ miles of river navigable from Guildford with 12 locks. That included no less than nine miles of artificial cut yet it is the Duke of Bridgewater who gets the credit for our first canal, in 1761.

With the final few miles still to be cut Sir Richard Weston died. It was May 7th 1652. The family chapel in Holy Trinity, Guildford is now the vestry; it had been founded by the ancestor who had built Sutton Place. Son George took over and the waterway opened the following year. All that engineering was achieved, by hand, in the same length of time as it is currently taking contractors to rebuilt one bridge (e.g. Plough Bridge, Hoe Bridge) with machines.

No known portrait survives of Sir Richard. He married Grace Harper of Cheshunt who gave him 14 sons and several daughters. The sketches above are to indicate costume only.

LOCKS

Locks come in two types: flash locks and pound locks. The first is a barrier of movable boards across the water to build up a greater depth behind it. The other is the result of placing two flash locks close together to impound water between them.

Flash locks operated by simply opening them and letting the boat speed through on the rapid release of water. Travelling up-stream was more difficult. It required a winch or a team of men to haul the boat against the outrush of water. Either way could be dangerous for boats, people and cargoes.

The pound locks on Britain's canals today are a great improvement. It has been suggested that they were introduced into England from Holland by Sir Richard Weston for use on the Wey. This is unlikely to be true. An Act of Parliament in 1623-4 permitted

what were probably pound locks to be installed in the Thames near Oxford but Exeter claims the earliest (1564-6) but there is some doubt whether this refers to pound locks.

Traditionally a Dutch invention, they probably originated in Italy by 1440. However, there's a story from Ancient Egypt, from the reign of Pharaoh Seneferu, that suggests those wonderful people had built a pound lock.

RIGHT:- Lloyd Hampshire taking the Iona down into New Haw Lock 12-9-1989

BARGES ETC.

Of the many types of craft that have used the Navigation the barges are the broad-beamed freight vessels. To call any other craft a barge is an insult and an unfortunate one if you say it to the face of a proud narrow-boat owner.

Barges are undecorated. They are also popularly believed to be devoid of living quarters but this was not always the case. The men may have been away for as long as a month, waiting for their cargo to be transferred from ships in London Docks, so living quarters were squeezed into the ends. There are plenty of photographs to prove it.

The last establishment to employ barges on the Wey was Coxes Lock Mill, Addlestone. Their use was discontinued in 1969 but revived again in 1981 when it was realised that it would once again be cheaper to bring corn from Tilbury Docks by water than by road. This traffic ceased in 1983 when the mill closed.

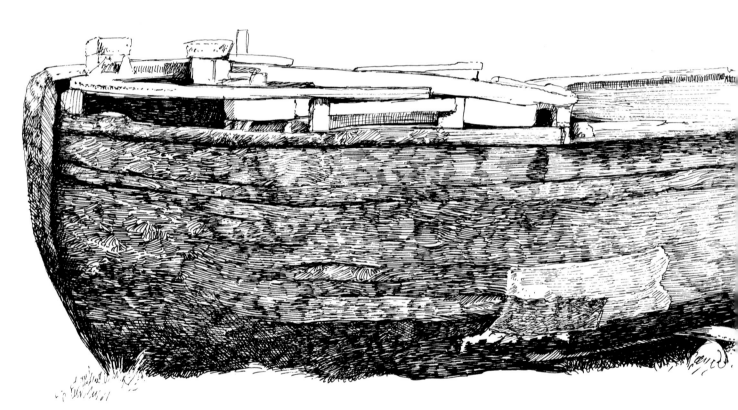

Like other waterways, the Wey developed its own design of barge, differing very slightly from those of the Basingstoke Canal. Photographs record craft of both designs on the Wey. They were 70 feet long or even a little more and about 14 feet wide. If that is difficult to imagine, it's the size of a lock.

The barge-building centre for the Wey was at Dapdune Wharf, Guildford. The last craft to leave the sheds was "Perseverance IV" which came in for rebuilding 1964-5. It made its last journey in 1968. There is a scale model of it in Guildford Museum. The barge-building shed was restored in 1989.

The National Trust wanted to show people one of the genuine Wey barges and after a long search two were located, sunk in the Thames mud. One was beyond redemption but a feasibility study suggested that the other, at Leigh-on-Sea, could be reclaimed. With the co-operation of the authorities at Southend this was achieved. Once it was made water-tight again it was floated back up the Thames and up the Wey to its birthplace at Dapdune. There it is now displayed, out of the water, to show both its great size and to help preserve it. It's the barge shown on these pages.

Barges leaving Guildford at four or five o'clock in the morning expected to be at Weybridge by four o'clock in the afternoon. That is, in time to bring back a return load. Sometimes horses would be taken direct to Weybridge by road to save time, in order to be sure of getting the load; no load – no wages.

Journeys right down to London Docks were not always popular as much time could be lost waiting for the load. Again it was the case that no load meant no wages. This was serious if the delay ran into weeks.

After their invention, steam tugs were used to tow barges up the Thames to Putney, Teddington etc. One tug could haul six barges. Two tugs in particular worked up the Wey aswell. One, called the "Teddington" hauled grain barges up to Coxes Lock Mill. The other, called "Oasis" was small enough to travel right up the Navigation to the wharves at Guildford.

As for the cargoes, corn and flour were the most important. There are said to have been more mills per mile on the Wey than on any other river. Coxes Lock mill was the most important.

Timber probably came second in importance with several timber yards on the waterway, such as Moon's at Guildford.

Then came vital supplies such as sugar, groceries, maize and barley together with raw materials such as coal for the gas-works, bricks for building, bark for tanning, rags for paper, kapok, linseed, monkey nuts and chalk.

Some of the barges carried 80 tons or even 90 on some occasions; usually much less. Hauling these by horse is a popular image but this declined during the 19th century in favour of man-power. Such men were called 'bow-haulers' because the tow-rope was fastened to the bow. However, local pronunciation made it rhyme with 'tow' and the syllables were run together to make it sound more like cricket 'bowlers'.

"Poling"
From a photograph kindly lent by J.C.M. Blatch Esq.

Sometimes only one man was used, sometimes a team. It depended upon the conditions. Going with the current was obviously much easier than pulling against it. Some of the men were from the barges while others spent the rest of their time working on the river in some other capacity. They moved a barge as fast as could a horse.

Moving the barges was always a highly skilled job. Floods increased the hazards of course as did strong winds which could swing the stern out across the water. A donkey or a pony was sometimes linked to the stern to prevent this. Work had to continue whatever the weather, even if the horses were up to their bellies in water.

Punting-style poles could also be used to move the barges but poling was discouraged because it cut up the bed of the waterway. Nevertheless there were occasions when it could not be avoided. Oars and sails were also used. Sailing was not popular because of all the low bridges which required them to be taken down. The load had to be less too; to compensate for the weight of the sails and their masts etc.

The first boats on the Navigation have gone unrecorded but the idea for the waterway came from Sir Richard's visit to Holland where, in the 17th century, artists recorded life with realism and so we can see what he had in mind: rowing boats and broad boats with sails.

Quick study of bow-haulers from an old photograph kindly lent for the purpose.

Eric Parker's "Highways and Byways in Surrey" of 1908 has an illustration of a sailing barge at Eastwood's Wharf, Weybridge. How anything as massive as a sailing barge could get up the Wey remained a secret through months of research until by glorious luck a photograph of one fell out of a pile of archives and when I picked it up the answer was written on the back!

Eastwood's needed to get their bricks for Weybridge from Kent and Essex so they had two "stumpy spritsail" barges made at Sittingbourne. One, called "Surrey" was made too big and would only fit the Wey if one leeboard was removed and stowed on deck. Evidently this is what is showing in my sketch from the photo'. It does not show in Thomson's sketch for Parker's book so he must have seen the smaller barge, called "Landrail".

Some of the main Wey barges had sails too but were only likely to be used on the Thames part of their journeys due to the quick succession of little low bridges over the Wey. They had a capacity of 65 tons but only carried 45 tons to Guildford due to the weight of the sails etc. Some branched off the Wey at New Haw to sail up the Basingstoke Canal to Woking. The sails were red.

Early in the 19th century evolved the craft we call narrow boats. They are entirely British, not found on the Continent, and come in several hundred regional variations. I was told very firmly not to call them long-boats as some people do. Long boats are Viking ships and modern boat people are not bent on rape and pillage. I was told that very firmly too.

Narrow boats worked in pairs: motor and butty, each weighing about 25 tons. Although only six or seven feet wide they're some 70 feet long so they were able to carry large amounts in their central holds. Just enough space was left on the motor for the engine room and on the butty for the living quarters. That living space was only six feet by eight feet yet whole families were brought up there.

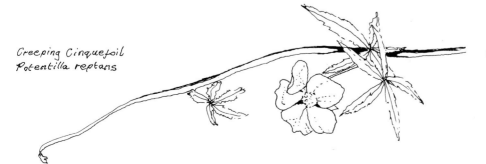

Creeping Cinquefoil
Potentilla reptans

Once used in anglers' bait to bring a good catch. They don't bother now and they don't seem to catch much either!

*Boat's eye view of the towpath 9-9-1989
Leaving Godalming Wharf with 'Baccarat'*

USING THE TOWPATH

The towpath is owned by the National Trust which invites anyone to walk it who is prepared to obey the bye-laws but anyone with destructive or anti-social tendencies will be asked to leave.

Cyclists are permitted providing they are not in large groups and that they give first consideration to walkers.

Horses are not permitted unless they're towing barges. Only a very short section at Byfleet, between Murray's Bridge and Dodd's Bridge is a bridleway.

Boats on the waterway need a licence from the National Trust.

PATH CONDITION

All stretches are used often enough for the route to be clearly defined.

From Walsham Gates down to the Thames the path crosses free-draining soils so it's fit for walking in shoes, even in winter. There may be a few muddy ruts to step over.

From Walsham Gates to Godalming the path crosses some heavier soils which, when wet, cling to footwear and can be slippery underfoot. Deep mud rarely forms.

It is of course a country path and walkers should expect such delights as overhanging long wet grass and stinging nettles. Too much trimming is detrimental to the wildlife.

MAPS

To really appreciate where you are and the setting of the Navigation, all the detail of an Ordnance Survey Map is needed.

Map 176 covers the mile or so from the Thames to Weybridge, then 187 covers the route as far as Walsham Gates after which the 186 completes the route up to Godalming in the 1:50 000 First Series.

Map 176: 072 655
to 187: 069 648

From Weybridge town centre, Thames Street leads to a wide pool in the Thames. Here, by D'Oyly Carte Island, Shepperton Weir provides a favourite place for canoeists. The island is where Rupert D'Oyly Carte brought his Savoy Operatic Company for meetings and rehearsals. It was his father's, bought as a future extension to his Savoy Hotel but his idea didn't appeal to the licensing authorities.

The quiet backwater through the trees on the left in the sketch above would not be recognised as the entrance to the Wey if it wasn't for the large sign.

The bank opposite was the site of Harmsworth Wharf. It took its name from A. J. Harmsworth who operated barges through here to join the Basingstoke Canal which he bought in 1923.

Just up Thames Street, the alley beside The Old Crown leads down to the towpath. Even before the Navigation was developed the Wey was a highway and in medieval times there were wharves along here.

The Tudor Palace of Oatlands stood a little further back. There's nothing to see of it now, on site, because when Crown property was in the hands of the Parliamentarians they put it up for sale on condition that whoever bought it must destroy it.

The spur of land on which the Harmsworth Wharf stood was once an island. Then, in the early 18th century, the present course was dredged out and the waste used to fill the old channel and so join the island to the mainland. Just below this point is the single-gate lock.

THAMES LOCK

Map 176: 072 655

Come in autumn when the sun glows through the golden limes and there's a whole rustle of colour to scuffle through around the lock, while a lingering whiteners of frost highlights the red tiles above the cream walls of the lock-cottage.

The collection of seven lock-cottages on the Navigation is of national importance. This one had to be rebuilt in 1975 but the National Trust preserved the appearance of the original. The adjoining stables are in its safe keeping too.

Since at least 1693 a mill has stood here on the island created by the overflow stream. At first it made paper but by 1720 had changed to working the local iron. When that ran out it became derelict, from 1817 until revived for crushing oil seed in 1842. Spectacular fires destroyed it in 1877 and again in 1963.

The story of the earlier fire and an illustration of the mill as it was in 1976 were included in the first edition of this book but have now been removed as the site was put up for residential redevelopment in 1989.

The footbridge over Thames Lock affords good views down onto the single gate lock below. It is closed when an extra depth of water is needed to enable craft to cross the bottom cill of Thames Lock. It was not needed until Sunbury Lock was rebuilt about 1800 and the level of the Thames was subsequently lowered. Indeed it was tidal right up to Walton-on-Thames until Teddington and other Thames locks were built and began controlling the water. Then the whole scene changed. The low-tide mud was no longer a feature and the banks began to be developed. The ancient willow beds were cleared and the local basket-making industry came to an end after a thousand years or so.

As you prepare to move off along the towpath look out for the native yellow water-lily. It is not a rarity but is often difficult to see closely as in most places it has to grow far out to find deep water. The Navigation, however, soon drops deeply allowing the lily to float close to the bank. That depth is for boats and so the lily gets shredded in propellers so look for it in the quieter places. It has had a wide range of uses in folk-medicine, such as easing diarrhoea, boils, ulcers and inflamation, but it's not for experimenting with.

THAMES LOCK
TO
WEYBRIDGE TOWN LOCK

Maps 176:072655 to
187:069648

The towpath introduces immediately all the variety of its long journey despite being so close to Weybridge town centre.

Trees border the Navigation with fields beyond. There are backwaters and weirs, boats and people and quietness too. A good range of plants and birds add beauty and interest to the scenery already made interesting by man.

There's always the pleasure of the unexpected: kingfishers flashing over an outfall stream and a woodcock being flushed out of the wet woodland margin made two visits particularly memorable.

The woodcock would once have been a delicacy on the dining table of one of the big houses through the former lands of which the Navigation now passes.

The land on the Weybridge side was Portmore Park, created in the 1670s by the 6th Duke of Norfolk, Henry Howard. It was set out by 1678 when John Evelyn, the diarist, visited.

The Duke's widow sold it in 1688 to King James II who gave it to his former mistress, Catherine Sedley, Countess of Dorchester. She married David Colyear, a Scottish soldier under William III who raised him to Baron in 1699, then Earl in 1703 – the First Earl of Portmore.

Woodcock
study
1988.

It was this Earl who bought a large amount of shares in the canal in 1723. He and his descendants, together with the Langton family from Lincolnshire, controlled the canal for over a hundred years. The 2nd and 3rd Earls ran into such problems that by 1793 it was necessary for the Chief Justices and Barons to appoint two additional trustees. It so happened that the two happened to be related to the Portmores. Well, well, well!

Soon a bridge comes into view. This was begun in 1939 but completion had to wait until after the Second World War. Beyond it lies a wide pool with the old town wharf on the far side.

No longer do walkers have to leave the waterside to walk round behind the weather-boarded shed as shown in this illustration from the first edition. The National Trust have restored the path to its former water-side route and built a new 'horse bridge' by which to reach the road which has to be crossed here.

Thus it now passes a vertical post on the corner which prevented the tow-ropes cutting the corner. The vertical roller on it was to save the rope from excessive wear and tear.

The lands on the tow-path side, Harum Court, have a history going back to the early Middle Ages. In 1732 they became part of the Portmore estates when the 2nd Earl leased them from the Dean and Canons of St. George's, Windsor. The house became derelict.

The 3rd Earl, the 'bad old Earl', disregarded the estates completely to spite his heir with whom he quarrelled. Thus in 1834 the Dean and Canons refused to renew the lease for the 4th Earl.

Of the actual houses nothing remains today.

Here the river and the canal enter the pool by separate arches and their waters reunited after following separate routes since Walsham Gates. There were wooden bridges and a ford since early medieval times. That changed with this fine iron bridge in 1865.

TOWPATH

WEYBRIDGE TOWN LOCK
TO
COXES LOCK

Map 187   068647 to 061641

The National Trust has parts of
Weybridge pool scheduled for
landscape improvement in
1990. Whether that will have
been achieved by the time
you visit, this next section
has already seen many changes
since the first edition was
published.

The Blackboy Bridge
in early spring.

The Navigation is raised well
above the road but down by
the road runs a backwater.
It's a branch of the River
Bourne but is no longer its
former self. Here, among half
sunk boats and floating
water lilies I sketched the
grey downy cygnets learning
about bottom-feeding. How
long their bodies were!

Blackboy Bridge took its name
from a statue in a nearby garden.
Formerly it was of brick but
was rebuilt in glorious concrete
in 1956 to take the gravel
lorries of the Thames River Grit Co.
It's owned by the National Trust
as one of their 'cross-over' bridges
to transfer the towpath from
one side to the other.

The use
of the canal-side for industry
along here is not new. There was,
for example, a water driven
sawmill here at the
beginning of the century.
The factories have not
only been rebuilt since
the first edition but
in some cases rebuilt
at least twice! Some
of their work has been
of national importance;
some of the buildings of
architectural interest.

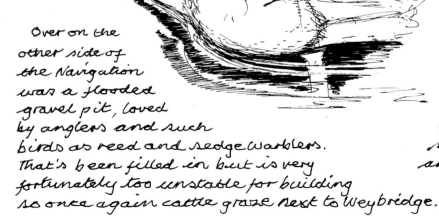

Over on the
other side of
the Navigation
was a flooded
gravel pit, loved
by anglers and such
birds as reed and sedge warblers.
That's been filled in but is very
fortunately too unstable for building
so once again cattle graze next to Weybridge.

Cygnet sketches 21-6-1981

This drawing from the Doorstep Book tried to capture one of those quiet early summer evenings when ever the mallard drake took time to loiter. Was an artist a danger or not?

The moorhen (right) was in no doubt. Human beings are supposed to keep moving and those that don't must be watched, preferably from the thickest vegetation available!

The Navigation is just as moody as the people who use it. The scene below records one of those endless summer days when it's too hot to do anything more than sit around. If you need an excuse then fishing or drawing serve very well! The site is beneath the railway bridge before Coxes Lock. The branch line, from Weybridge to Chertsey, opened in 1848. It was extended to join the main line at Virginia Water in 1865-6.

E. Hawkins.

COXES LOCK MILL

Before it closed
April 1983

The most important mill
on the Wey Navigation.

The date of founding the mill is unknown but obviously after 1653 when the canal opened. It was probably in the 18th century when Daniel Lambert of Chertsey leased the land to Alexander Raby, a South Wales ironmaster of local importance. He was adding to the mill in 1783.

It soon became the most important mill in the local iron industry. The waterwheel hammer beat out the iron with 45 blows a minute, earning it the name Hackering Jack. This enraged the adjoining landlord, the notorious 3rd Earl of Portmore....

He set out to stop it and nothing would deter him. Thus in 1808 Raby sold out to John Bunn who fared no better and so converted to flour milling in the 1830s.

Tales of silk weaving are true but the experiment was short-lived.

By the end of the 19th century new milling technology was putting many a rural watermill out of business. It was either get modern or get out. At Coxes Lock they decided to get modern and rebuilt: firstly in 1901 and a second building in 1906. The work was by Christy's of London and became the most important industrial architecture of its time in the county.

Listed for preservation, it is these buildings that have been retained and converted into residential use.

Water power had given way to steam and that to electricity. In the mid 1960s the great wheat silo was added ~ 137 feet high. In 1969 a lower flour silo was built. In 1969 also, the barge traffic ceased in favour of road haulage. It was one of 22 mills operated by Allied Mills Ltd, producing 60 tonnes of flour a day. By the end of the 1970s they realised it would once again

be cheaper to bring in the Canadian corn from Tilbury Docks by water than by road, so barge traffic was reintroduced.

Inside it was surprisingly quiet and very clean; all flour dust was extracted from the air and mixed with other by-products to make animal feed. Nothing was wasted; the aim was to reach 75% extraction because that was the potential of the corn grains. For that, each grain was opened out between fluted steel rollers: a Swiss invention and indeed this most modern machinery in the mill (left) was of Swiss manufacture. In contrast, the sifting was achieved on the oldest working mill machinery in the country (above). It was nearly a hundred years old and still working perfectly.

White flour, in five or more grades, was the chief product, followed by the browns, such as wheat meal and wholemeal. Bran came third. These were distributed over a wide area of S.E. England, from Hastings to Southampton, up to Newbury and back to London.

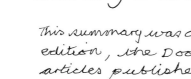

This summary was compiled from entries in the first edition, the Doorstep Book and Seen In Surrey articles published by the Surrey Advertiser.

COXES LOCK
TO
NEW HAW LOCK

Map 187: 061641 to 055630

Beside Coxes Lock is the mill pond, as seen in the drawing below, made from the top of the great wheat silo before that was demolished.

The best time to see the pond is on a clear winter's afternoon when a red sun hangs just over the water, bold behind the stark silhouettes of the alder trees on the banking between the pond and the canal.

See how the water flows into the pond when the lock gates are closed but when the gates open a cill prevents all the pond draining out. In this way the pond drove the mill irrespective of what was happening on the canal. This simple procedure was a great improvement on other places where millers and canal folk wrangled in court over who had first rights to the use of water. Nowadays it's the preferred habitat of coots and great crested grebes (above) which find the rest of the waterway too confining for comfort.

Looking in the general direction of Byfleet, across the fields at Wey Manor. The mill pond is on the right with the canal to the left and extreme left is surface flood water in the fields.

The path soon becomes very rural, bordered by lush vegetation, full of wild flowers and, on a calm evening in early summer, rich with the heavy scent of elders.

It was on a cold grey afternoon though that I recorded Mute swans mating, for the Doorstep Book. The cob had all his feathers up and bore down on the pen with loud whistles. Biting hold of the base of her neck, he tried to force her under water. She fled up and down the water with much flapping and splashing but he was equal to that. Next she tried zig-zagging up and down the banks, yapping like a Yorkshire Terrier, but he only became more determined. Even racing under low bushes didn't dislodge him. Several times he mounted her until finally, with great modesty, they mated under a laurel bush. Afterwards he washed himself very thoroughly, even to the extent of forcing himself under water. That took several attempts as he was very buoyant. Other swans, including grey cygnets had joined in with whistling, whirring, snorting and yelping. Mute by name but not by nature! You never know what a expect along the towpath; it's a very special part of Surrey.

The scenery along here has changed. The overgrown hollows beside the wide bend were Hersey's watercress beds until 1963. Bates' Timber Yard has been replaced by the housing of Bates Walk. The farmland has been reworked as a P.Y.O. fruit and vegetable centre; its old white farmhouse in the distance was the home of the John Bunn who worked iron at Coxes Lock Mill from 1819 to 1829. His house has some of the rarest Dutch architectural features in the country, leading some to wonder whether it was built by a Dutch engineer brought over by Sir Richard Weston to advise on the building of the canal.

NEW HAW LOCK
TO
PYRFORD LOCK

Map 187 : 065631 to 054592

However appealing the idea of horse-drawn **boats** may be, it's not very practical today at places like New Haw Lock where there's no towpath under the bridge and so traffic has to be halted.

"Baccarat" on the
Anniversary Run
12·9·89

Halt! Horse crossing!

The bridge ahead carries the A318 over the Navigation and when you climb the path up onto it, there's New Haw Lock beyond. This has been an important bridge point for hundreds of years.

This open sunny spot attracts many visitors, especially as there are shops, the White Hart pub and a car parking bay nearby. There's also a slipway for getting craft in and out of the water, which provides added interest to watch.

The pub and the bridge were for long the focal point here which, before modern development, was the top corner of the vast Woking Heath. Indeed 'haw' meant flat marshy land beside a river in Anglo-Saxon times. The earliest mention of this haw is in a will of 1187.

Looking at the census returns it would seem that the White Hart was built between 1851 and 1861 but there was an earlier version somewhere nearby, going back to the 18th century at least — not only as a pub but providing the families on the canal with their groceries etc.

During Restoration.

The lock cottage is a Listed building, variously dated to the 1780s or about 1810.

A gas cylinder explosion inside in 1982 shifted it somewhat! It wasn't destroyed, however, so after five months work costing £12,000 it was made safe and stable and ready for use again.

Early photographs show that the banking between it and the canal is not original but added during this century.

Eventually the tree-bordered path passes under a railway bridge which came into use in 1838 to carry the London and South Western Railway towards Southampton. It was Surrey's first main line railway.

Nowadays trains terminate at Waterloo but that terminus did not open until 1848. Before that, trains terminated at Nine Elms where there was a vast area of marshalling yards, locomotive sheds and riverside wharves.

London, unlike most European cities, had separate terminals for freight and passengers.

This particular bridge was enlarged in 1884 when the railway was expanded to four tracks.

Horse-power and helmets and
trials of skill to attract a
female; knights and squires
and teenagers; perhaps fairs
haven't changed so much
after all!

Fair At New Haw.

On its way to the railway bridge the path runs alongside the scene below. Here the canal is raised well above the level of the land which must have been quite an engineering job back in the 17th century. All this was then wet heathland. Now it's the housing of New Haw where owners are happy to have the canal at the bottom of the garden – providing it stays there! No one wants to be inundated with millions of gallons of water so the National Trust has to monitor the banks carefully, looking for any signs of weakness.

By the late 1980s the National Trust felt that erosion had gone far enough and the site came in for restoration work to reinforce the banks. Hopefully readers will appreciate that such work, carried out by the National Trust, is vital. However, there was a fuss here because trees had to be felled, even though it was planned to replant the scene. It's a pity active conservation work has to be carried out in the face of opposition. Nature reclothes a scene so fast that a few months of disturbance is surely worth years of further enjoyment – and safety. It all costs thousands of pounds so it's not undertaken lightly.

THAMES LOCK
WEYBRIDGE
3M

THE NATIONAL TRUST

Signposts on a waterway — that's not something you see every day! This one was added by the National Trust.

Between the motorway viaduct and the railway bridge is the entrance to the Basingstoke Canal which opened in 1796 and brought increased traffic to the lower reaches of the Wey Navigation. It was much longer, stretching thirty seven miles through Hampshire farmland to Basingstoke. It was originally important for bringing out farm produce to the London markets, when roads were too poor and distances too great. Then the railways came into being and could do the job even better. Still the canal lived on, bringing supplies to the army camps at Aldershot, until 1921. After that only the first few miles were in regular important use commercially, as barges took coal up to the Woking Gas Works.

When that ceased the canal became derelict. In 1966 a Society was formed to try and restore the waterway and so begins a magnificent story of achievement, as obstacle after obstacle was overcome. When the first edition of this book was written the canal was due to reopen. Now, eight years later, that is still the case, as even more obstacles have had to be overcome. In readiness, a new footbridge has been added to link the towpaths of the two waterways. In former times the towing-horses had to be ferried across by boat.

Watch out for Long-tailed tits along the twiggy waysides.

BASINGSTOKE CANAL
GREYWELL 3¼M

OFORD   12M
GODALMING   16½M

The Navigation was the first important change to the Wey Valley landscape. Then the railways caused an even greater re-shaping. Then the M25 out-did the lot! All three can be pondered here.

Soon you'll find the canal broadens out, by the boathouse. Here barges were turned round after using Byfleet wharf just ahead.

That there should be boating here is the perpetuation of a condition imposed by Frederick Cornelius Stoop, who bought the land from the canal owners for £50. He lived at nearby West Hall and was a great benefactor to Byfleet.

Two to go!
~ an unexpected gesture captured just as unexpectedly on film as I recorded the 'Anniversary Run' negotiating the M25 viaduct. It was easy for the barge but not for the horse; the supports for the viaduct were built too close to the edge of the water, so blocking the towpath. This caused much throwing of the rope backwards and forwards while the barge progressed along under its own momentum — not for the first time on the journey.

West Hall, Byfleet
R Hewkin RA 1983

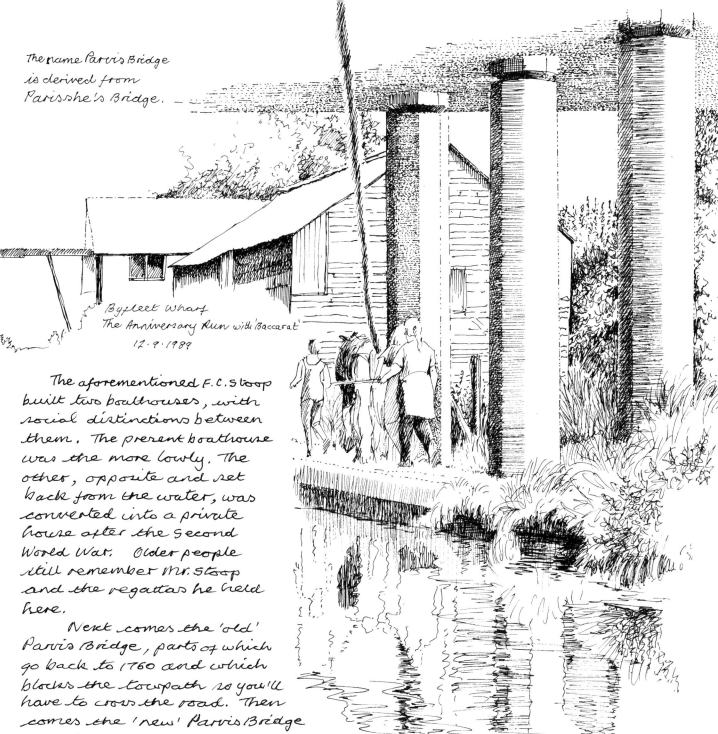

The name Parvis Bridge
is derived from
Parisshe's Bridge. —

Byfleet Wharf
The Anniversary Run with 'Baccarat'
12·9·1989

The aforementioned F.C. Stoop built two boathouses, with social distinctions between them. The present boathouse was the more lowly. The other, opposite and set back from the water, was converted into a private house after the Second World War. Older people still remember Mr. Stoop and the regattas he held here.

Next comes the 'old' Parvis Bridge, parts of which go back to 1760 and which blocks the towpath so you'll have to cross the road. Then comes the 'new' Parvis Bridge carrying the A245 over the M25. It's the supports for this which can be seen in the accompanying sketch. Between the bridges nestles all that remains of Byfleet Wharf.

The story of this site isn't easy to retrieve today. There were, most probably, six little mills here; one or more dating back to 1780, and one of these survives as the weatherboarded building (now owned by the National Trust and let for income). It was working as a grist mill within living memory. There was at least one cottage here too but that has now gone.

Along the opposite bank is the edge of West Hall where Stoop lived and where at least eight gardeners maintained the grounds. The Head Gardener was a Mr. George Carpenter who bred more new strains of apple than anyone else in Surrey, between 1915 and the 1930s. Six were released onto the general market.

The pollarded plane trees illustrated opposite stretch out over the canal from West Hall.

Approaching open meadowland, you come upon the first of a series of picturesque little bridges. This one is Murray's Bridge, belonging to West Hall. It links the grounds with Murray's Lane which runs up to the interesting medieval church at Byfleet. It's the only church in Surrey built throughout with windows having Y-tracery. The lane was planted with an avenue of horse chestnut trees, now cut through by the M25 although the gap through these fine mature trees has been bridged. They've given it the local name 'Conker Arch'.

Byfleet

St. Mary's Church.
Byfleet, Surrey.
B. Hawkins 1980.

The Murray part of the name comes from R.H. Murray who lived at West Hall before Stoop. On June 1st 1869 Mr Murray invited the whole parish to lunch on his lawn. This was part of a Dedication Festival to celebrate the completion of the new south transept on the parish church. This was built by the noted Victorian architect Henry Woodyer but this is not a notable piece of his work.

The Dedication Festival became an annual event. It was not always held at West Hall but was, however, in 1892 because that year Murray hosted a new attraction — a bicycle race!

Just as the venue varied so did the date, after 1889, and by that year the name had changed to Parish Day. The event, under that name, is still held every year, alternating between the recreation grounds at Byfleet and West Byfleet.

The short meadowside walk from Murray's Bridge to Dodd's Bridge is the only length of towpath that is a public bridleway. Dodd's Bridge is another of those lovely little brick structures and this one is safeguarded in the ownership of the National Trust.

Moorhen

By now you'll be reaching what some people might call "real" farmland with cattle in waterside meadows — and hay making. When the sketch above was made in 1981 hay making was declining rapidly in Surrey and that might well have been the last time the meadows were so harvested. It's now being said that farming as we know it will very soon disappear from Surrey north of the Downs.

It was Sir Richard Weston's interest in irrigating hay meadows that led in part to the creation of the Wey Navigation.

One of the unexpected pleasures of walking through here was to find shaggy long-horned cattle in the fields. It was feared this would end when the M25 sliced through the fields but the Highland Cattle were soon back.

Until 1989 the motorway had only three lanes on this section and traffic was so often at a standstill that the peace was disturbed less often than expected.

Fears for the cattle were also generated at this time because the farmer closed his butcher's shop. People realised suddenly that Byfleet without Derisley's the butchers would never be quite the same. The Derisley family originated from Diss in Norfolk, with Robert Derisley working Church Farm at nearby Wisley. He was joined by his brother Lloyd in the 1870s and it was Lloyd who began the butchers side of things in the 1880s and opened the shop in 1894.

At the time of revising this book, 1989, the cattle are still there.

Byfleet 1981

Byfleet 1981

PYRFORD LOCK TO WALSHAM GATES

Map 187 : 054592 to 050578

Passing the fine old coppice stools of hazel, the path arrives at The Anchor, at Pyrford Lock. The old pub with oil lamps has long since been replaced by the popular modern pub of today. The name is most likely to derive from the 'anker' unit of measurement of drink (8½ imperial gallons) It's a word from the Dutch which was sometimes rendered as 'anchor'.

The towpath crosses the road and the road crosses the canal by humping over another of those little bridges and then doubling back on itself. Just watch the faces of unsuspecting motorists! This is the only public road bridge owned by the Navigation. The lock is on one side and on the other was stabling for the tow-horses, now replaced by the pub patio.

Soon the towpath twists between trees. It shouldn't! Think what would happen to the tow-ropes! The path used to run on the canal side but severe erosion has removed the land. It shows so clearly why the National Trust are forced to protect some banks with steel sheeting.

The journey is now through a landscape that is as close to being woodland as any stretch on the route. The canopy of mature trees and thick layer of shrubs and undergrowth beneath make this a rich habitat for birdlife. Half a mile of it, between the canal and the river, has been bought by the National Trust recently as part of its Wey Valley Protection policy.

The Hawfinch (above) is no doubt an under-recorded species, being quiet and secretive, living high in the tree tops where it is difficult to see. A rare record of one was made along here on February 4th 1985.

The Redpoll (right) was first recorded for this area in the 1955 Wisley Bird Report, ahead of the general increase that occurred in the early 1960s. Look for it feeding on the birch and alder cones here, from November to March. It is still not a particularly common bird although there is a peak in numbers every few years. To see the weak winter sun catch the pink and crimson in its plumage is worth waiting for.

The path soon reaches Pigeon House Bridge and a straight stretch of canal which marks the site of a former wharf. The nettles in the adjoining space mark the site of the wharf cottage and stables. They were evidently built of black weatherboarding.

Here they unloaded corn for Ockham Mill and took the flour away. The footpath off to the left, towards the river, follows the course of the former cart track to the mill. Indeed, by peering over the river footbridge the foundations of the earlier cart bridge can still be seen in the river bed.

Following this route across the fields, away from the canal, walkers arrive at the attractive hamlet around Ockham Mill, with its mill stream and Weeping Beech tree.

Another new arrival in the 1955 records was the Siskin (bottom left) which also feeds on the birch and alder cones along here. Local flocks vary from 20 to a few hundred but beside the Wey the flocks are usually small. They are still easy to overlook as they prefer to feed high in the tree tops. If you have disturbed they are readily recognised for flocking into swirling, twittering masses that reel around the tree tops. For a closer view try an early morning visit after a stormy night when you might find them down on the path getting the fallen seed.

Ockham Mill was rebuilt in polychrome brick in 1862. It is the finest industrial building of its time associated with the Wey Navigation.

Next comes Pyrford Place, once belonging to nearby Newark Priory. At the Dissolution it became Crown property and was in due course leased by Elizabeth I to Lord High Admiral Clinton whom the Spanish Ambassador described to Philip II as being "a very shameless thief, without any religion at all."

Alder catkins

The summerhouse of Pyrford Place stands on the bank of the canal. Pause and look at that too long and a passing local is liable to tell you Elizabeth I flirted in there with the poet John Donne.

It's an entertaining notion but the summerhouse was not built until the end of the 17th century; long after the Queen had died. Don't be too disappointed though; both people did figure in a romantic drama from here.

Elizabeth did visit here because after the Admiral she leased it to her Latin secretary, Sir John Wolley. He was married to one of the Queen's ladies-in-waiting, Elizabeth More of Loseley, near Guildford.

The Mores of Loseley were her most trusted agents in Surrey and were in attendance upon their Queen when Sir Robert Dudley, Earl of Leicester, knighted Elizabeth More's father here at Pyrford.

By this time Sir John had died and his widow had married again — Sir Thomas Egerton, who later became Lord Chancellor. He son, Francis, from the first marriage, had inherited the estate. He was a friend of John Donne so when Sir Thomas needed a secretary it was John Donne who got the job.

Thus he was present at the knighting ceremony and there he spotted Ann More, a Loseley heiress. She noticed him too but he was just a commoner and she was far from it. They didn't allow that to make any difference!

John Donne wrote to her father that they had been secretly meeting each other in London and that they were now married! "I acknowledge my fault to be great," he wrote but "we adventured equally." He begged that Ann should not "feel the terror of your certain anger."

Donne had time to think on this while he served his prison sentence! Friends at Pyrford eventually succeeded in negotiating his release into their custody and so John and Ann began their married life here at Pyrford Place.

Mr. G. Bailey outside his
Walsham Lock Cottage, 1983.

Meet Mr. Bailey – as indeed you may, for the stretch from Pyrford up to his lock cottage at Walsham and so up to Newark Lock is his 'patch'. He's one of the full-time members of a whole team of lock and weir keepers employed on the Navigation.

Apart from ensuring public safety and correct usage of the waterway, their most important job is as Water Controllers. The Wey has a greater catchment area than most British rivers and all the water gets funnelled down through the Navigation. Twenty nine sets of regulating gates have to be attended, often on private land with the active help of private owners.

Mr. Bailey has spent all his working life "on the land". He knows it, he loves it and now he helps care for it. Like all the other Navigation men he has great knowledge and a wealth of tales to draw upon; oral history garnered from visitors to Walsham who relate their memories of the place as it was in earlier days. Of course many tales are only believable to the teller! Others have truth – that the hollows by the gateway to Walsham were created by squatters' camps while others lived in old railway trucks in the cottage garden, until the trucks were set on fire to drive them out.

Baby blue Tits in
their nest hole.

39

By Walsham Gates
C. Hawkins 1983

WALSHAM GATES

Map 187 : 050578

To my way of thinking this is one of the most attractive and interesting spots on the Navigation; quiet and peaceful out in the flood meadows of the River Wey.

When the canal was built, fields of vegetables for the London markets were at Battersea and Lambeth. By the late 18th century such fields had been pushed out to Camberwell and Brixton. Nowadays they're out here at Walsham where a winter walk on the Pyrford side takes you through the leek harvest.

Leek field
Walsham 1983

Walsham, as seen above, shows us the early look of the canal. Here is the last of the original locks, not only grass-sided but square from the days before long barges. The bridge, complete with shallow steps for horses, is dated 1785.

Sun behind
Walsham
B. Hawkins
1984.

Following the towpath you find the bridge and the lock on your right and the cottage on your left with the River Wey surging along behind and below it. By 1989 the cottage was showing its age and also slipping down the bank towards the river.

The National Trust spent thousands of pounds underpinning, restoring and bringing it up to modern living standards yet to passers by it looks just the same as it always has. That, of course, is exactly what the National Trust intended.

Rounding the cottage and passing a little promontory, the path takes you over a long weir down which surplus water plunges to foam off as the River Wey on its separate course to Weybridge. The channel was improved in 1932 by some of the Welsh who had come to Surrey seeking work during the depression years. Floods across these meadows were then so common that a boat was kept moored here for the lock keeper to ferry the children across to school in Ripley — and back again.

frog

Above :-

A tricky few moments on the Anniversary Run — persuading the horse to follow the towpath on its traditional route over the great weir. Untrained horses don't like water rushing under their feet and it was not an everyday experience for this horse but nevertheless it was crossed with dignity. The horse was 'Domino'.

For obvious safety reasons horse-drawn boats were not towed across the water at the top of the weir. However, it forms a wide pool (shown below) and creates the problem of how to get the barge across, from the sketching point to the canal entrance at top left.

Crossing the pool was achieved by speeding-up the horse along the towpath until the barge had enough momentum to propel itself across. Steering and assistance could be achieved by poling. The horse was disconnected at the last moment of course.

Coming the other way was more difficult as the horse might over-run off the promontory into the pool. That was overcome by looping the rope through a horizontal pulley fixed to the promontory and trotting the horse back in the opposite direction.

2.2.83

During the 1989 Anniversary Run these problems were avoided by using an engine! The motor-powered "Lynx" accompanied the "Iona" to assist where modern bridges etc would obstruct the tow-rope and is seen here towing the Iona into the pool to reach the canal gates.

The lock gates at Walsham are rather special. For an explanation see the section on Worsfold gates.

Left — the pulley referred to top right. It is not always on show as some people delight in ripping it out of the ground.

WALSHAM GATES
TO
NEWARK LOCK

Map 187 050578 to Map 186 042575

29·10·1982

Beware ~ the route now becomes more rural. Be prepared to walk through wet grass if it has been raining and in high summer the rain may have bent over the tall grasses to soak your legs.

The path is well defined and where it has been worn bare it may be sticky underfoot in winter for the soil changes now from sand to loam.

29·10·82

Along here kingfishers have posed for me to sketch them! The two little sketches were a splendid consolation on a cold wet day which made drawing anything difficult. Remember it is on the specially protected list of the Wildlife and Country-side Act (1981) so it is an offence to disturb one in the breeding season.

The Route is shown in the sketch on the next page. It was made from a photograph I took from a light aircraft in 1988. It looks a long way from Walsham at the top to the lock at the bottom, hidden behind the trees round the Mill House but it doesn't take very long. It depends how enthusiastic you are about all the wildlife you can spot on the way ~ from birds, bugs and butterflies to wild flowers. It's a lovely walk through the fields and trees yet so close to Woking.

44

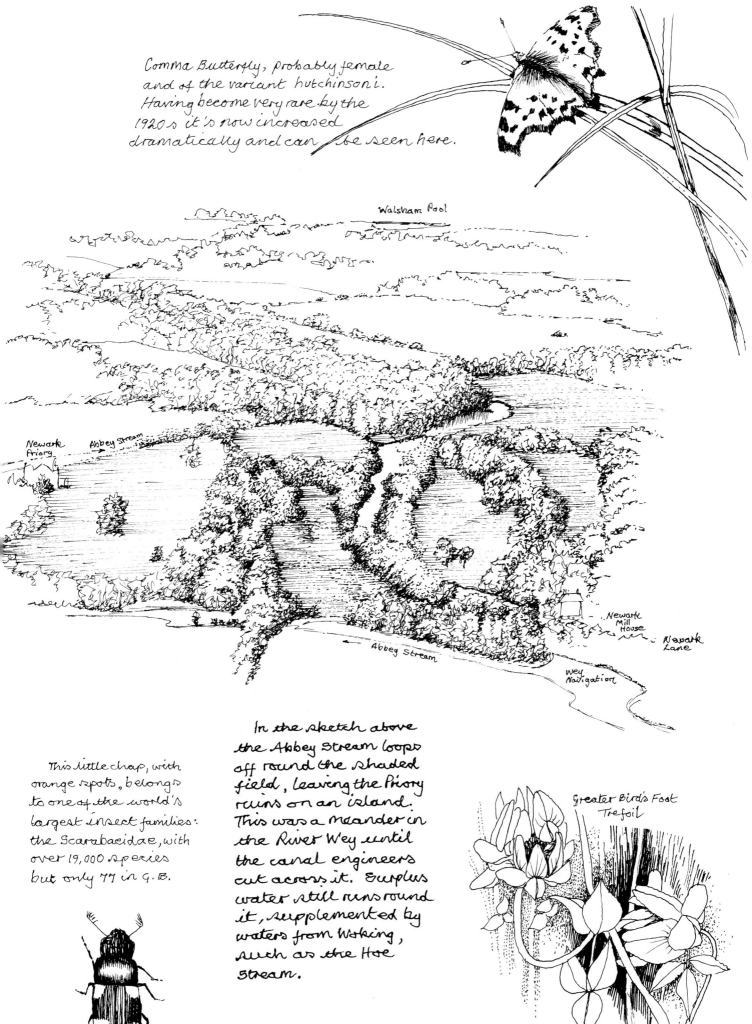

Comma Butterfly, probably female
and of the variant hutchinsoni.
Having become very rare by the
1920s it's now increased
dramatically and can be seen here.

Walsham Pool

Newark
Priory

Abbey Stream

Newark
Mill
House

Newark
Lane

Abbey Stream

Wey
Navigation

This little chap, with
orange spots, belongs
to one of the world's
largest insect families:
the Scarabaeidae, with
over 19,000 species
but only 77 in G.B.

In the sketch above
the Abbey Stream loops
off round the shaded
field, leaving the Priory
ruins on an island.
This was a meander in
the River Wey until
the canal engineers
cut across it. Surplus
water still runs round
it, supplemented by
waters from Woking,
such as the Hoe
Stream.

Greater Bird's Foot
Trefoil

45

NEWARK LOCK TO PAPERCOURT LOCK

Map 186: 042575 to 034568

A short walk on a hard path takes you from Newark Lock up to the lane from where you can look back upon the scene on the right.

Adjacent is the site of the former Newark Mill, sometimes called Pyrford Mill, which burnt down over thirty years ago. The mill house survived. This is thought to be one of the mill sites recorded in the Doomsday Book.

The road is Newark Lane, from Ripley to Pyrford, with a small car park here. It's too small for busy sunny Sundays so don't bank on finding a space.

From the lane the towpath crosses great open fields to Papercourt Lock so be prepared for wet grass.

The fields are popular with people who enjoy the wide open spaces. It's one of the most spacious spots on the route.

Before entering the fields it's possible to walk a little way along the lane to get a view of the ruins.

NEWARK PRIORY IS ON PRIVATE LAND WITH NO PUBLIC ACCESS.

What you see is part of the church; the rest of the monastery has been robbed for building materials. Even so, what remains is some of the most important architecture of its date in Surrey.

Lunch stop in the Newark fields with 'Domino'
Anniversary Run 11-9-1989

Newark Priory was a House of Austin or Augustinian Canons, known as Black Canons because they wore a black hooded cloak (over a white surplice over a black cassock).

The Order arrived in Britain in the early twelfth century and spread rapidly till there were over 200 Houses. When this particular one came into being is not clear.

According to a document of 1312 it was founded by a Bishop of Winchester. This was most probably Godfrey de Lucy who granted land, before 1204 when he died.

Perhaps this early venture failed because the House was refounded. That was by Ruald de Calva and his wife Beatrice de Sandes, during the reign of Richard I (1189-1199).

The location of the first House is unknown but was probably elsewhere in the district because the name Newark is believed to have derived from 'new works'.

Canons were not monks; they were priests. Thus they did not have to stay at one Priory and their life was less austere than that led by other Orders.

Stories from the Priory are scant but we can imagine the bustle before a bishop's inspection! It didn't always work. In 1387 Canon John Chesterton failed to cover his tracks well enough. The Bishop's Commission removed him into custody, at Merton Priory, for his "excesses".

This leaves us to conclude that to sin in moderation was acceptable! Indeed this seems often to have been the case. Many medieval charges read "too much", "too many" or "too often".

In this case, the Prior, Alexander Culmeorston, resigned, supposedly infirm.

The most notable contribution made by Austin Canons was in the provision of medical care.

They treated sufferers with the dreaded leprosy and of importance to us today, they founded St. Thomas's and St. Bartholomew's Hospitals in London.

Their Rule was based upon the 109th letter of St. Augustin.

Two grass-lovers: the
Field Bindweed and the
Wall Butterfly.

The Bindweed, such a
curse in the garden is a
delight in the wild with
trumpets ranging from white
to pink and white stripes
with a darker eye. The only
useful member of the
Convolvulus family is the
Sweet Potato.
The Wall Butterfly is only
sunbathing, as it loves to do.
Its caterpillars eat the grasses
the Bindweed scrambles
through, such as Couch Grass.

Brambles attract Painted
Lady Butterflies through
the summer to feed on
the nectar and then
on the sugary juice
exuding from over-
ripe fruit.
   The caterpillars
prefer to much
away on thistles
and nettles.

   Newark Priory in
the background: the
ruins of the church
with south transept to
the left and presbytery
to the right.

Young cattle in their shaggy winter coats beside the footpath through Papercourt Farm

The towpath runs through the back of this scene to the lock cottage beside Papercourt Lock, indicated in the background. Footpaths can be taken across to Tannery Lane. It can be muddy in winter.

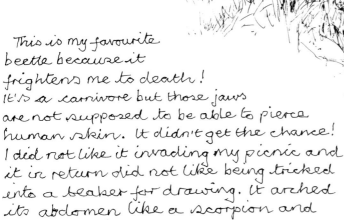

This is my favourite beetle because it frightens me to death! It's a carnivore but those jaws are not supposed to be able to pierce human skin. It didn't get the chance! I did not like it invading my picnic and it in return did not like being tricked into a beaker for drawing. It arched its abdomen like a scorpion and squirted stinking yellow fluid at me. Serves me right I know!

The beetle is called a Devil's Coach Horse. His scientific name is more splendid — Ocypus olens. He's got twelve relatives in Britain but this one is the largest, reaching 32 mm. I've drawn him bigger, then he can frighten the lot of us!

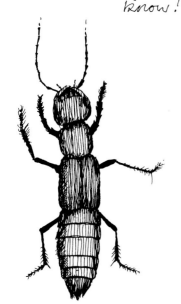

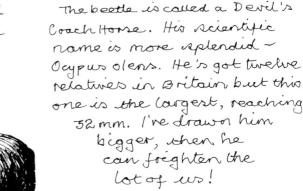

This is Herbie. He deserted the cattle to come and see what I was drawing — him!

Papercourt Farm, built in the 1660's with richly coloured brick was the Manor of Papworth. The name was in existence in 1204. It had become Papercourt by 1686.

It is connected with Sir Richard Weston who founded the Navigation. The Manor was granted to a branch of his family by Ruald de Calva of Newark Priory fame. These were the Westons of West Clandon. The Lord of that Manor, in the early 17th century was Edmund Slyfield and he passed it to Henry Weston of the Ockham branch of the family. In 1711 John Weston sold it to Sir Peter King of Ockham and its connection with the canal's founder was lost.

No book about the Wey Navigation would be complete without mention of the Giant Balsam that is spreading rapidly along the waterway. It was introduced from the Himalayas to Britain in 1839. Here it grows six or seven feet high but in its homeland reaches ten feet and it's only an annual! It springs up in great thickets to produce banks of bloom in summer, ranging from white to pink to crimson. Wild flower books list it as Impatiens glandulifera but horticulture books call it Impatiens Roylei. It's already got many English names.

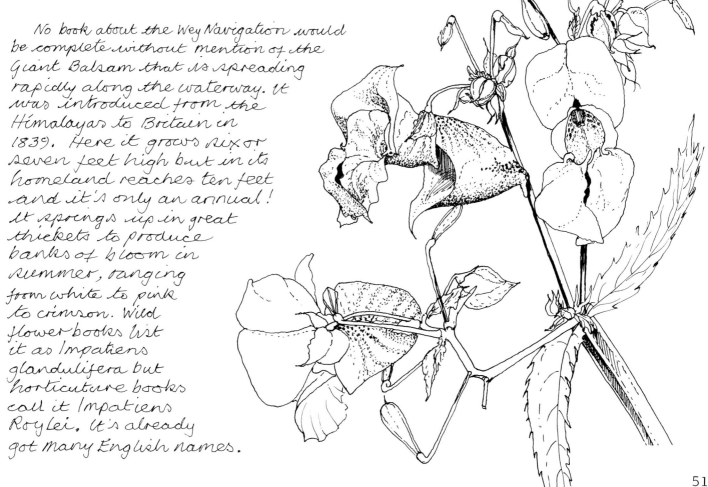

PAPERCOURT LOCK
TO
WORSFOLD GATES

Map 186 : 034568 to 016557

After a broad sweep through the meadows the towpath rises to cross the Navigation at Papercourt and then cuts straight through the trees — the trees that form the top border to the fields in this 1988 aerial view.

From the towpath there are views out over the fields. The A247 from Old Woking to Send can be followed directly across this page.

Above here the A247 meets the mini-roundabout in Old Woking. The High Street crosses this page to run into Westfield and so round to Kingfield. These two fields, now built all over, went with the Broadmead (illustrated) to make up the three great Open Fields of pre-Enclosure days.

This writing covers the roofs of Old Woking, built above the flood level, but the setting sun on a hazy afternoon has not rendered them clear enough to copy accurately from the photograph.

The A247 runs into the trees and over Cartbridge in the join of these pages. You would expect to see the roofs of Send at the bottom of this column but at this angle they are hidden in what looks like extensive woodland. Only the gravel pits break the trees to show up on the photographs taken.

The Navigation doesn't show up anywhere. The river does. It comes in on the right to the industrial complex in the centre, to the mill pool (vertical shading) in front of Unwin Brothers' printing works. Then it cuts through the trees to the B382 and turns left out of the sketch at Broadmead Bridge.

From the river on the right another waterway flows right across the landscape, a field's distance from the trees. This is the Broadmead Cut, made in the 1930s to reduce flooding. What a wilderness of alder and willow groves this must all have been when man first arrived. The Broadmead was then created and farmed communally as part of Old Woking's 'Open-Field' system. It's an impressive survivor and can be explored by public footpath from the towpath.

LOOKING SSW.

Part of ruins of Woking Palace.

To walk around the old Woking district is to explore a land of kings, for this was a royal manor, although often in the hands of court favourites. For example, Edmund Beaufort (died 1455) paid a nominal rent each year of one clove gilliflower (a carnation).

When it came into the hands of the great Lady Margaret Beaufort, it reached fresh royal prominence for her son took the crown of England on Bosworth Field and became the first of the Tudor monarchs as Henry VII.

All the Tudor monarchs came here. It has even been claimed that Queen Mary I was born here and not at Greenwich.

It was Henry VIII who rebuilt the Manor as a more sumptuous palace. Today it is in scant ruins out in the Wey meadows on private land.

It is mentioned here because there has been pressure to grant public access. Already some groups have been shown around and the promise of greater access has rumbled through the local press. Perhaps by the time you read this a (lengthy) detour from the towpath to visit the site may be possible.

These two illustrations have been borrowed from the 'Royal Tapestry' book.

The illustration right was the scene beside Woodfold Gates. The Great storm took out some of the trees here, as elsewhere en route.

Tudor Childhood.
(for the rich!)

Worsfold Gates
Wey Navigation, Surrey.

G. Hawkins 1982

After passing a shimmering
fringe of reeds (Phragmites
communis), which is becoming
increasingly scarce in Surrey,
and then passing a rustling
border of exotic Bamboos, the
towpath reaches Cartbridge.
Here the A247 has to be
crossed on a dangerous bend
to reach the waterside track
up beside the New Inn to
Worsfold Gates.

The bridge (right) is scheduled for
rebuilding so be prepared for changes here.

'Domino' on his best behaviour again!
Recording the television news.
Anniversary Run 11.9.1989

56

WORSFOLD GATES
Map 186 : 016557

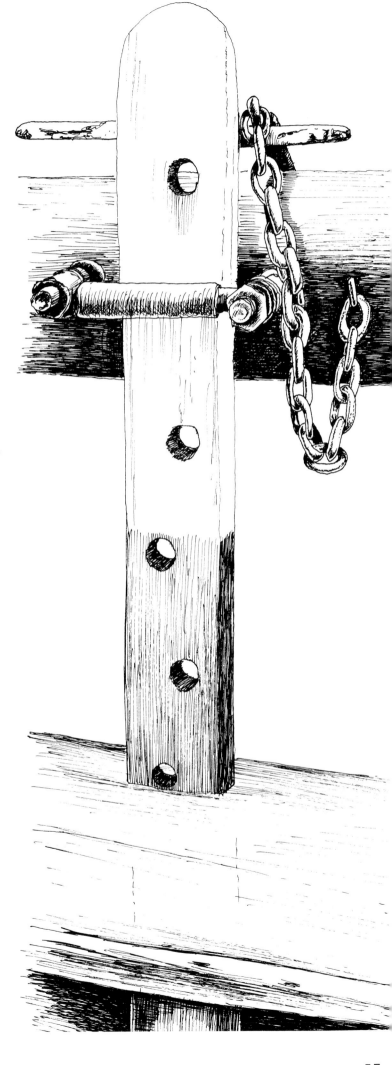

The New Inn attracts extra visitors to this spot, where they can wander along the waterside track to the gates (lock).

These lock gates are not the only survivors of their design in Britain, as has been claimed. There is another set at Walsham.

Their special feature is that the 'paddles' below water are raised and lowered by hand without the use of gear wheels. They are held in place by the pin in the illustration.

This is presumed to be the design used by Sir Richard Weston. The two sets have survived because they haven't had to be forced up and down against water pressure, using a crowbar. Here, and at Walsham, the pressure is the same both sides as the canal is allowed normally to flow through. Only when floods surge down are they closed, to force the excess into the old river course and so out into the meadows. There it can be held until it is safe to return it to the canal, in a controlled way using sluices. If need be, the fields can be flooded to act as reservoirs.

At Walsham flood waters are forced over the weir into the river and so to Weybridge. There the extra flood waters do not cause the last section of the canal to burst its banks because there are overflow channels to take excess off to the Thames, avoiding the last locks.

WORSFOLD GATES
TO
TRIGGS LOCK

Map 186 : 016557 to 013549

The black weather-boarded building of the sketch above is the lock cottage, so very different from all the others along the Navigation. It's the last survivor of a once popular style along the canal.

The notion of a timber frame clad in tarred boards began in Georgian times, around the S.E. coasts as a development from fishing boat construction. The idea spread widely inland and pitch gave way to the fashionable white lead paint. It also spread abroad to the Eastern United States. Nowadays both black and white boarding are back in fashion.

Common Newt.

Beside the towpath by the cottage is a rustic timber and tile building such as can be seen all over rural Surrey. This one is of interest for it is thought that it was built at the same time as the canal to serve it in some capacity. It still does. This is the base from which the maintenance teams work.

4.
12.6.77

Opposite : summer gales sweeping up the willow branches. Here the natural river runs off at the left to journey out round Old Woking before rejoining the canal below Papercourt Lock. Here too, by the path, you'll find the remains of a former horse-bridge that took the towpath over to the other side.

Worsfold Gates
E. Hawkins
1983

After the confines of Worsfold the pathway runs out into the meadows again, tilting gently down to the river, catching the warmth of any sunshine and encouraging people to loiter a little.

Looking up the valley you see the higher ground running down to the meadows from the left with attractive views of Send church out on one of the spurs. Below it runs the river coming to rejoin the canal just below Triggs Lock. Here the new towpath had to be raised upon a concrete causeway to avoid the wet.

The meadows are indeed water meadows and can be very wet in the winter. Attractive as the church may be, a winter visit by footpath over these meadows may turn out to be a most memorable experience of deep mud and surface water! However, it is beautiful through here in the winter so try exploring when severe frost is locking mud and water solid. Forget the cold; enjoy the blue sky and winter sunshine.

Here the river and the canal share the same bed except for two small loops of river that go off on the other side. Cutting the necks of these meanders was one of the acts of the 1930s Improvement Scheme. I wonder why Sir Richard Weston's workers didn't do it in the first place? The whole idea generated great hostility in many of the landowners.

The towpath used to run along the far bank until the cuts were made, hence the need for the horse-bridge noted back at Worsfold (to return the path to the present course).

Send.

The presence of a church is recorded in the Doomsday Book (1086) but the present tower, nave and chancel are replacements built about 1200. In the 18th century the height of the tower was raised by nine courses of bricks and their tile capping when the battlements were repaired. It's a fine focal point in the landscape.

St. Mary's Church, Send, is the only medieval rural church that's at all close to the Navigation, which indicates what a wet wilderness the whole lower valley must have been when communities were first founded. Even today the village of Send is safely up on higher ground, leaving the church group as an isolated hamlet.

True, St. Peter's, Old Woking, is on the bankside of the original river but the lower Wey does not become a feature of a sequence of riverside villages complete with ancient bridges, as can be found in many other valleys. That at least left the route clear to make navigable.

The soft ground suits birds like these green plovers or lapwings which gather food there. The rough pasture with rush clumps and bare spaces suits their needs for breeding too but changes in farming and too much human interference do not suit it so nationally the population has been declining. On a good day you can still see them through here — and hear them.

61

TRIGGS LOCK
TO
BOWERS LOCK

Map 186: 013549 to 012529

This is one of the longer sections, being about two miles. Soon after Triggs there are no access points along the route so it is either a case of keeping going or doubling back. The journey is through fields and trees; rough countryside in places and English parkland in others. In winter it can feel remote and desolate and slippery underfoot in places. In summer it's a joy of flowers and butterflies but not everyone will enjoy the long grass if it's wet. The trees attract woodland species of birds like this greater spotted woodpecker which can be heard calling its warning 'spink.. spink' call or seen retreating in its loopy flight pattern.

The lock cottage was built about 1820 and came in for extensive renovation in 1987 but this was done so well you'd hardly notice. The lock keeper was an important man here because he had control over the level of the water. This was achieved by adjusting an unusual arrangement of paddles in the lock gates to allow surplus water through. Only since the Navigation has become the property of the National Trust has the tumbling bay been built to provide a surer and self-regulating means of controlling the level.

If you've walked this far from the Thames you've covered just over 9½ miles and so you're halfway along the total length of the towpath. That was not so in Sir Richard's scheme of course, for that only reached as far as Guildford. The extension on up to Godalming was added in 1760.

Here at Triggs was the site of Sir Richard's own watermill.

sainfoin

After Triggs Lock comes Wareham Bridge, one of twenty four Navigation bridges owned by the National Trust. It takes the footpath from Sutton Green over to Send church but nowadays Sutton Green has its own church. Glimpses of Send church through the trees keeps the eye alert to the left all along this stretch, especially when a low sun is catching the tower.

The canal is skirting the fields of the founder's estates at Sutton Place. The white clover is a common summertime flower and it was here that Sir Richard Weston introduced it into British farming, to enrich the soil with nitrogen and the hay with protein. That's why, I've been told, it is still called 'Dutch' clover sometimes; he collected the practice on his visit to the Low Countries. However, this claim is challenged in favour of him having commercialised the red clover, which he certainly grew here and is still a common wild flower.

Dutch Clover.

One that is not is the sainfoin which he also brought into agricultural use. Today it's a rarity, found in only five locations during the Surrey Flora survey.

We know about his farming ideas because he wrote a book about them while he was out of favour :-
"Directions for the Improvement of Barren Land" (1645, 1651 and issued again in 1652.

Soon the canal confronts the driveway to Sutton Place and turns sharp left (Whippet's Turn) to run alongside it before turning sharp right and under the private Broadoak Bridge of the drive. On that last bend is a roller, stationed originally to guide the towropes. Another, plus brackets for two more, can be found under the bridge.

Right on the bend surplus water cascades down over a weir, as the natural river, diverting from the canal. It runs out past Send church to rejoin the canal below Triggs Lock, as already noted. This weir is part of Sir Richard's original scheme. Indeed he is attributed with being the first in England to build tumbling bays and other ornamental cascades. The additional cut into it, from the other side of the bridge, was added during the 1930s improvements.

At present there is no public access to Sutton Place which is private. However, it has been opened to the public in recent years and may be so again.

The Navigation now runs through Coopers Meadow beyond which is Bowers Lock.

A glimpse of Sutton Place where Sir Richard Weston was born in 1591. Henry VIII visited in 1533 and two years later began the Anne Boleyn adultery trials. They found Sir Francis Weston guilty and he was executed; so was Anne — the first queen of England to be charged with, and executed for, adultery.

ENJOYING
THE
BIRDLIFE

A wide range of species occur through here, as there is a range of habitats. The waterside attracts the reed bunting (right). The mature trees of the park provide nesting holes for the nuthatch (left) and coal tit (below).

BOWERS LOCK
TO
STOKE LOCK

Map 186 : 012.529 to 002516

When first exploring the Navigation this was the section I left to last, thinking, so wrongly, that it would have been spoiled by all the nearby building shown on the map. Don't make the same mistake! It's one of the very attractive stretches.

Winding curves keep you full of anticipation as to what's round the next bend. The broad fields of the previous stretch change smaller more intimate water meadows.

Parts of the meadows are still boggy so there is a greater range of wildlife. The trees close in, enriching that range further and including the lovely pollarded willows shown in the sketch below.

6.4.83

Brave the winter cold and you'll find a few snowdrops. The first warmth brings the celandines and the white violets and, for the sharp-eyed, the moschatel, so tiny and green. Then comes the lady's smock and so into the full richness of summer, until floating leaves burnish the waters of another autumn and the alder catkins turn over once again to hang through the cold.

This stretch is part of the original three miles cut by Sir Richard in 1618-19 for flood control and irrigation, before the long distance scheme was initiated.

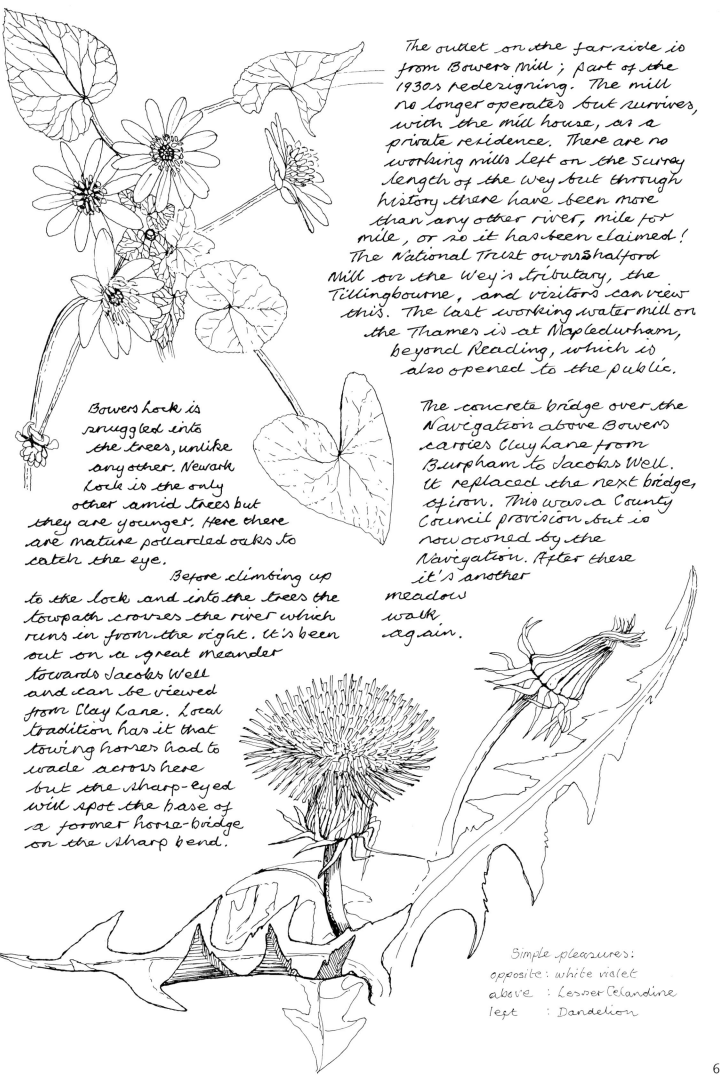

The outlet on the far side is from Bowers Mill; part of the 1930s redesigning. The mill no longer operates but survives, with the mill house, as a private residence. There are no working mills left on the Surrey length of the Wey but through history there have been more than any other river, mile for mile, or so it has been claimed! The National Trust owns Shalford Mill on the Wey's tributary, the Tillingbourne, and visitors can view this. The last working water mill on the Thames is at Mapledurham, beyond Reading, which is also opened to the public.

Bowers Lock is snuggled into the trees, unlike any other. Newark Lock is the only other amid trees but they are younger. Here there are mature pollarded oaks to catch the eye.

Before climbing up to the lock and into the trees the towpath crosses the river which runs in from the right. It's been out on a great meander towards Jacobs Well and can be viewed from Clay Lane. Local tradition has it that towing horses had to wade across here but the sharp-eyed will spot the base of a former horse-bridge on the sharp bend.

The concrete bridge over the Navigation above Bowers carries Clay Lane from Burpham to Jacobs Well. It replaced the next bridge, of iron. This was a County Council provision but is now owned by the Navigation. After these it's another meadow walk again.

Simple pleasures:
opposite: white violet
above : Lesser Celandine
left : Dandelion

STOKE LOCK
TO
MILLMEAD LOCK

Map 186 : 002516 to 996492

WARNING

At Stoke Bridge walkers
    have to cross the A320.
At Woodbridge the By-pass
    has to be crossed.
In town centre there is a
    very short break in the towpath:
    just continue ahead towards
    the left side of the church.

Stoke Lock is the earliest
pound lock in Surrey,
being part of Sir Richard's
initial three mile
scheme of 1618-19.
    That was for agricultural
rather than transportation
purposes. Claims that this
pound lock is the earliest
in England are weak.
Records reveal locks being
built along earlier schemes
although they do not tell
us any details of design.

    Built into this lock is a
large grey dressed stone. This
is pointed out as possibly
having been part of Henry VIII's
Palace of Oatlands at Weybridge;
helping to confirm the story
that when the palace was
destroyed, by order of the
Puritan Parliament, the
materials were bought by
Sir Richard for building
the canal.
Certainly Tudor
bricks have been
found behind
at least one
lock.

Mallard

Stoke Lock is surprising for
being so high above the
river in its meadows. This
was so that the grass
could be irrigated by
deliberate flooding according
to Sir Richard's original
scheme. Water overflowed
the canal to be guided
down across the fields
into the river. That
raised ground temperature
just enough to ward
off spring frosts and
thus promoted early
pasturage when the
cattle were at their leanest.
There was no winter feed
available, except hay,
until Sir Richard
introduced turnips.
That idea was taken
up later by Viscount
'Turnip' Townsend in
Norfolk and it's
he who gets all
the credit for it!
    Sir Richard's scheme also
irrigated the hay crop for
a better yield, maybe even
two in a season.

Today the river can still
flood here and then it's
a good time for birdwatchers:
seeing which species have
come to join the gulls to
scavenge for drowned beasties.
Seeds also float to the surface
and attract dabbling ducks.
The teal is particularly fond
of dabbling around in surface
water over fields.

Soon Stoke Bridge comes
into view : a County
Council job of 1926.
    Beside it is Stoke
Mill, being restored
at the time of
this revision.

CH.
9·8·1977

Stoke Mill is the grandest piece of Victoriana along the Navigation. Unfortunately it was wrapped in plastic sheeting for restoration when it needed sketching for this edition. Below is the sketch from the first edition, made on a bitterly cold day.

There is a long tradition of milling at Stoke but it is often difficult to differentiate the mills in old records because "mills" was used in relation to the grinding stones or the water wheels rather than the building. Thus a site or a district could have more than one mill without having more than one building. Both corn and paper have been recorded at Stoke Mill at various times.

To grind corn safely requires power at a constant rate but operating locks interrupts the flow of water and thus the pressure. Millers and bargees did not co-exist happily. Disputes between them were endless, especially where the river worked the mills before canalisation. Court action was frequent and the bargees had often to pay the millers for the water. Such was the case at Stoke. In 1832 millers at Stoke, Newark and Woking agreed on the "Millers Indenture" which formalised working practices. Weybridge followed in 1849.

Mills that came into being after canalisation had their terms set out by the Navigation Authorities right from the start.

Teal
CH.

Having crossed the A320 you find where the Navigation was cut away from the river about 1650. Sir Richard's earlier cut of 1618-19 began where the Rowbarge pub now stands. The Navigation made use of only the first half mile of this.

This pub name is the only obvious commemoration of canal life. It's one of only five pubs on the waterside. Once there were eleven serving it.

The closeness of Guildford is by now obvious yet the walk is still through meadows. The back gardens of houses in Weyside and Stoughton Roads run down to the opposite bank. The straight stretch before Wood Bridge is an alteration demanded by the new A3 but the course had also been altered back in 1856 when the railway from Woking arrived.

There is no towpath under the bridge so walkers have to cross the by-pass. That highlights the impossibility of reviving the horse-drawn boats, however attractive the idea might be. The traffic has to be halted by the police, as was done for the Anniversary Run but which would not be acceptable on a regular basis.

These first three lines of writing cover what would be Woodbridge Road if the aerial sketch were extended. Even the original colour photograph is confusing as the familiar landmarks on the ground lose their distinctiveness from the air. New features appear boldly, such as the cricket ground, over which I am now writing!

The towpath, running beside Woodbridge Meadows, enters the illustration at the bottom of this page and passes under the grand brick viaduct. This was built in 1885 by the London and South Western Railway to carry their line from Guildford to Hampton Court. It's Guildford's finest piece of railway architecture.

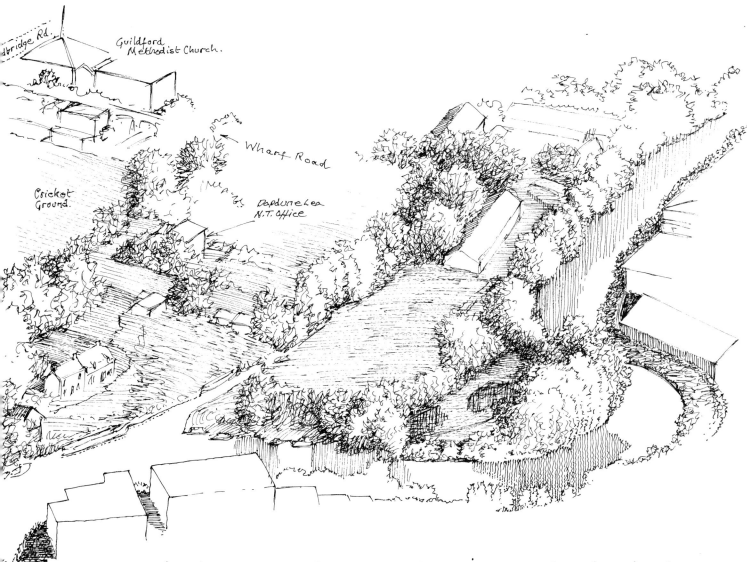

The following labels appear on the drawing:

...bridge Rd.

Guildford
Methodist Church.

Wharf Road

Cricket
Ground.

Dapdune Lea
N.T. Office

The writing is now over the new Riverside Business Park. The important feature is the inlet off to the right from the neck of the meander. Here, on the far bank, is Dapdune Wharf, which was the former barge building centre. The last barge to leave here was Perseverance IV in 1965, which had been in for a refit.

The scene has changed since photographed as the National Trust has undertaken an ambitious restoration scheme with a view to developing a Wey Heritage Centre.

Under the trees, brambles and nettles important discoveries were made which have now been uncovered and restored.

These included not only the dock which has been cleared and put back into use but the former graving shed which has been rebuilt. Up on the bank they restored the forge where the great iron nails were made that held the barges together. Materials relating to the steam bending of the stout oak planks came to light too. All that was needed was an example of a Stevens barge that had been built here. Two were traced but both were sunk in the mud of the Thames estuary. One was beyond redemption but the other .....

(next page bottom left)

HALEY'S
PATEN...

A barge jack

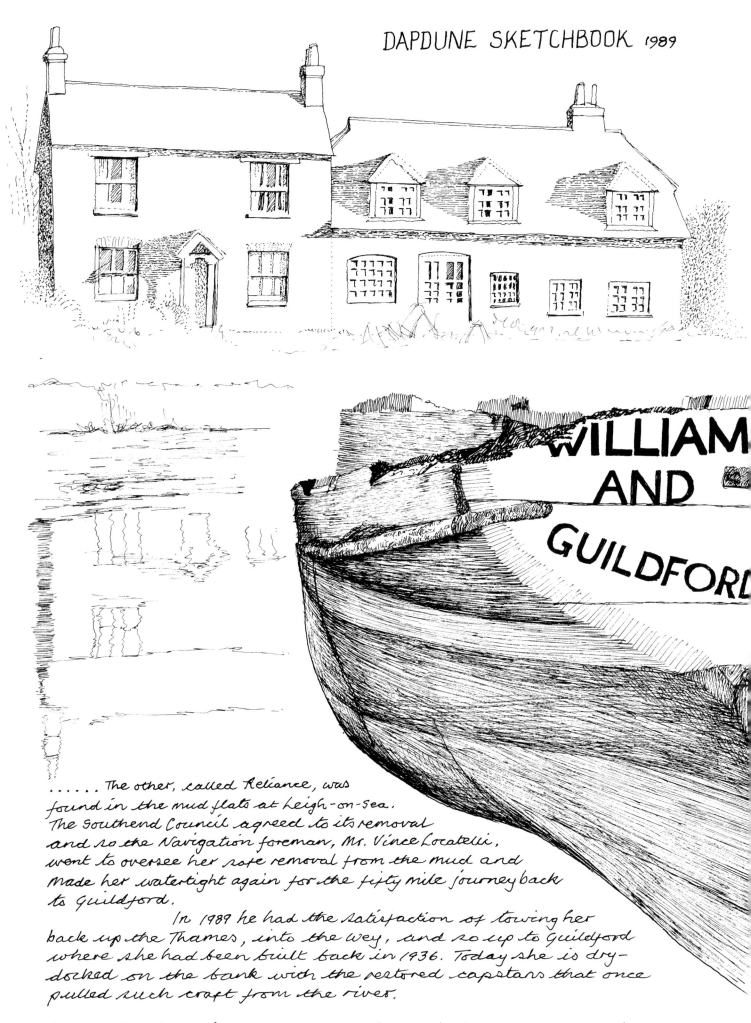

...... The other, called Reliance, was
found in the mud flats at Leigh-on-sea.
The Southend Council agreed to its removal
and so the Navigation foreman, Mr. Vince Locatelli,
went to oversee her safe removal from the mud and
made her watertight again for the fifty mile journey back
to Guildford.

     In 1989 he had the satisfaction of towing her
back up the Thames, into the Wey, and so up to Guildford
where she had been built back in 1936. Today she is dry-
docked on the bank with the restored capstans that once
pulled such craft from the river.

Length: 74ft (22.5m); beam 13ft 10in (4.22m). Could carry over 60 tonnes.

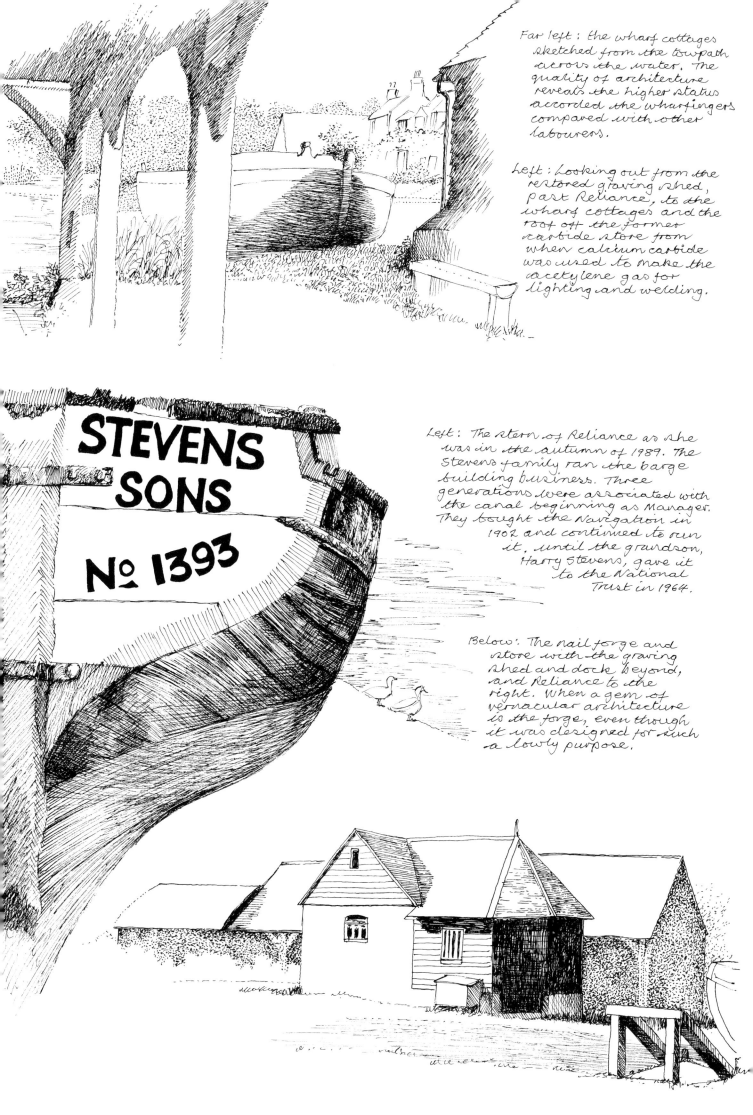

Far left: the wharf cottages sketched from the towpath across the water. The quality of architecture reveals the higher status accorded the wharfingers compared with other labourers.

Left: Looking out from the restored graving shed, past Reliance, to the wharf cottages and the roof of the former carbide store from when calcium carbide was used to make the acetylene gas for lighting and welding.

STEVENS
SONS

Nº 1393

Left: The stern of Reliance as she was in the autumn of 1989. The Stevens family ran the barge building business. Three generations were associated with the canal beginning as Manager. They bought the Navigation in 1902 and continued to run it, until the grandson, Harry Stevens, gave it to the National Trust in 1964.

Below: The nail forge and store with the graving shed and dock beyond, and Reliance to the right. When a gem of vernacular architecture is the forge, even though it was designed for such a lowly purpose.

DAPDUNE WHARF
is reached via Wharf Road
off Woodbridge Road
on the other side of the river.

TO CROSS THE RIVER
use the footbridge on the
aforementioned railway
viaduct, or, Walnut Bridge
ahead — the pale streak
across the sketch below.

THE NATIONAL TRUST'S
NAVIGATION OFFICE is
also at Dapdune, in the
large Victorian house that was
built originally for Mr. Stevens'
sister.

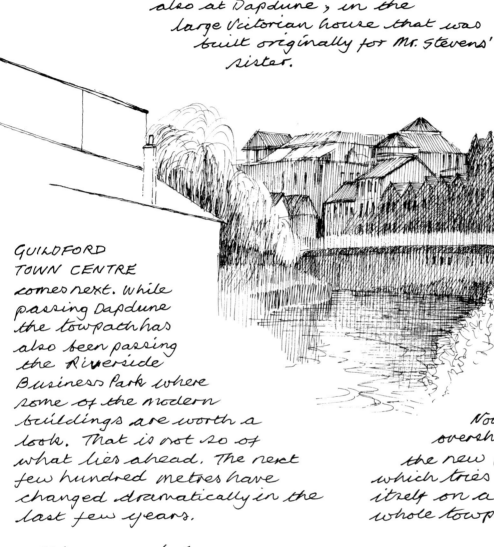

GUILDFORD
TOWN CENTRE
comes next. While
passing Dapdune
the towpath has
also been passing
the Riverside
Business Park where
some of the modern
buildings are worth a
look. That is not so of
what lies ahead. The next
few hundred metres have
changed dramatically in the
last few years.

Now they are
overshadowed, literally, by
the new (1989) Guildford House
which tries to make much of
itself on a cramped site. The
whole towpath is overshadowed
as the Trust's
property is
walled in
by modern
development
with a
singular
lack of
imagination
regarding the
full potential
of the
riverside
site. This
is fortunately
a short
section.

Old commercial
buildings still
stand, built
attractively
round the curve
with a partly
gabled outline
jutting into
the sky. They
were enough to
provide variety
and give a
sense of place.
All they need is
a good clean.

That dreary section is short but it does highlight the National Trust's difficulty in protecting the environs of such a narrow property; only 45m wide on average.

Soon the towpath is lost altogether and walkers have to head across the hard surfaces towards the church of St. Nicolas — and that is not a spelling mistake!

All at once things get much more interesting. Firstly, over the river, beside the bridge you'll spot this intriguing building. It's a crane, probably 17th century.

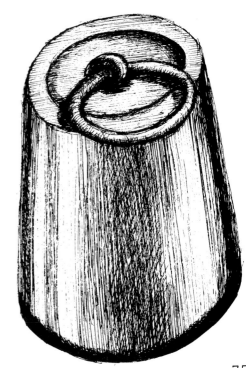

The only other such cranes are at Harwich and Kings Lynn. It was operated by one man (possibly two) treading the 18ft. treadwheel inside the building. It's geared to lift about one ton, no more, despite popular tales and was still being so used within living memory.

It has the unusual distinction of being listed as an ancient monument.

A much quoted statistic is that in 1794 the town levied a 1d toll on every load at the wharves to raise funds for paving the streets. It took only a year to raise the necessary £124-12s-6d. Very approximately that's 6-8 loads per hour and as a load could be as much as 60-80 tons we get a very rough notion of the working life of waterway.

Right: a barge weight, used for weighing the loads.

Echoes of the past: Harnessing the tow horse in Millmead. Anniversary Run, 10.9.1989. ("Baccarat")

The stretch without a towpath was the site of Crooke's Brewery — a reminder that this was once the commercial heart of the town, with breweries, wharves, warehouses, timber yards, iron works and so forth. It was cramped, dirty and noisy. It was also busy; through here squeezed the main route to cross the only bridge.

"Alice in Wonderland". Sculpture in the grass by Town Bridge to commemorate Lewis Carroll's association with Guildford.

Barge traffic came up as far as the bridge, until 1760. In that year An Act of Parliament sanctioned extending the Navigation another four miles up to Godalming. Thus the stone arches of the medieval bridge had to be altered to allow barges through.

As a road bridge it became so inadequate that Onslow Bridge was built, a little downstream, in 1882 and a new traffic system was created.

That was just as well too on February 19th 1900 floods swept wood from Moon's timberyard (now site of Debenham's) and piled it against the arches of the old bridge until the pressure destroyed it. It took two years to rebuild; it opened again February 5th 1902.

By 1985 the Town Bridge needed major repairs but there fortunately retained the original appearance. It's now for pedestrians only. How small it seems!

Beside it the medieval church of St. Nicolas survives in part; a very small part. Most of it dates from 1875.

Otherwise the Victorian scene along the riverfront has been swept away, so we walk by riverside lawns and weeping willow trees, looking across to Debenham's and the theatre instead of a timberyard and ironworks. Then there's the mill to note of course.....

..... canoes cross the pool where fish were farmed in the 18th century and the mill was rebuilt in 1760 (later additions carefully matched) when part of its use was for pumping water. It was as a pumping station that Guildford Corporation took it over and installed new pumps in 1896.

It also worked corn and cloth. It was bought by Henry Smith in 1624 and he devoted the income to relieving the local poor. This obviously suited the Corporation very well so in 1665 they ordered all local clothiers and meal men to use the Town Mill.

Today it's used by the Theatre.

MILLMEAD LOCK
TO
ST. CATHERINE'S LOCK

Map 186: 996492 to 996477

Millmead
was once a
mead or meadow
where cloth from the mills was put
out to dry. Meadows still abut it;
quite surprising for being so close
to town centre but then this
short stretch is full of surprises
and contrasts.

The path is still
running through trees - trees that
provide the best autumn colours
anywhere on the towpath. The
drooping branches of the beeches
shed a thick layer of floating
gold on the water, to be
curled back in the wake of
a boat, like a scene in a
giant creamery.

Boats are very
important since their licenses
contribute to the maintenance bill
fund and there were some 2,000
craft registered in 1989.

Everyone can embark upon
the waters here, courtesy
of the Guildford Boathouse.
Organised excursions
are offered for those
who don't wish to man
their own boat. One

of the craft so employed
has been named after Harry Stevens.
Alternatively, you can enjoy watching
others "mucking about on the river"
as per the sketchbook doodles on
these few pages.

Travellers of a different kind
are the seasonal birds, following
the north-south corridor of the
valley on their spring and
autumn migrations. Just as
the waters get funnelled through
the gap in the hills here so do
the birds. One of the many
regular visitors to arrive in
autumn for the winter is
the redwing, shown above.
At first they're to be
seen in flocks around
autumn berries,
such as the
hawthorns' by
the waterways.
Then they'd
search the
meadows, if
unfrozen,
for worms etc. Frost
drives them to gardens.

So it's suddenly out into fields again. This isn't just "nice" but vital. These meadows can be flooded deliberately to reduce pressure in the river and so reduce the flood risk in Guildford itself. They have even been flooded in winter to give ice skating facilities!

The sketch below shows the meadows flooded in early autumn, beyond what looks like a causeway but which is in fact the Navigation bank. The true waterway course is thus in the foreground.

The ruin on the hill beyond is St. Catherine's Chapel.

Even out here it hasn't always been so pleasantly rural. There was an important trade in chalk and Guildford Rowing Club now has its building on the site of Davis' Wharf from where the chalk was boated out. It was used as fertilizer and in the production of cement.

It's not the chalk you're likely to notice so much as the golden sands of St. Catherine's Hill where they spill down to a former ford in the river — dredged out when the Godalming Navigation came into being after 1760. The town is thought to be named after it: the golden ford (gold – gild – guild). It is certainly a stark feature for people to remember.

The ford was replaced by a ferry, still marked on out-of-date maps, but which has long since ceased to function. In the 1980s the County Council provided a footbridge, to carry the North Downs Way over a footbridge which met with unexpected hostility, on aesthetic grounds.

The North Downs Way follows, where possible, the route on earlier maps called the Pilgrims' Way. Although a route passed through here, the 'Strata de Geldone', the notion of it being a pilgrims' route is a fanciful notion dating only from last century. There is no evidence for it. Calls for us to imagine Chaucer's pilgrims on it are nonsensical – who would have travelled from London to Canterbury via Guildford?

To leave the boaters and climb the hill is worth the pant. The view is refreshing after the confines of Guildford. Look back on the town, as in the sketch below and the castle can be picked out as the left hand building on the skyline. From here the choice of site looks obvious whereas in Guildford itself the growth of the towns masks the value of the site. The castle keep is what you see and that was probably built before 1173.

Below the hill, meadows (flooded in the sketch) spread over to the tree-hidden village of Shalford. Look for the church spire.

The chapel was built in 1317. The ruin sits grey and brooding on its hilltop or shining gold and white in the sunlight.

Imagine those rubble walls newly plastered over, the windows complete with tracery, the corner turret and the pinnacles rising high, and the sun catching a fresh coat of whitewash. What a gem this must have been.

Prayers were offered for a safe crossing and thanks given for having had one. A sister chapel of St. Martha offered the same opportunities, on the opposite hill beyond the ford. The two saints are said to have built the chapels with only one hammer between them. They tossed it to each other across the valley – no doubt with loud warnings of "Coming Over!"

It's a shame to ruin that smile but the two buildings are of different dates!

There's truth in the dangers of the crossing though. The river's catchment area is unusually expansive, being some 30 miles by 35 miles with rain being fed into the river by some 182 tributaries. The

rush of water below this hill after a heavy storm must have been prodigious in the days before flood control measures were taken. Even so the risk of floods today has to be monitored carefully and is a real threat.

Leaving the hills behind, it is only a short walk to St. Catherine's Lock. Before that the river comes in from having a good old wiggle through the meadows over to Shalford and back. There, up to 6 million gallons of water a day (1989 figure) for domestic supplies.

These meanders were by-passed by the Godalming Navigation so the walk from the confluence up to the lock is by artificial cut.

Monkey Flower

ST. CATHERINE'S LOCK
TO
UNSTEAD LOCK

Map 186: 996477 to 992460

You're right out in the fields again and don't you know it where there's a biting winter wind and the ground is waterlogged! It's a beautiful desolation though. Then there are those warm days in early summer when it seems to be all flowers and butterflies. A glance over the shoulder back to St. Catherine's on the hill (as in the sketch below) makes you glad you're not trudging round Guildford.

The first feature for many walkers will be the lock cottage. Don't look for it by the lock though. It's further on where the river sluices out through the "Riff-Raffs" to Shalford. Thus it was built for a weir keeper rather than a lock keeper. That was for £239 back in 1909! It is, therefore, much younger than the others noted.

Next, the route is crossed by the railway from Reading via Guildford out to the Redhill junction and so into Kent. Built in 1849, only ten years after the main lines began pushing into Surrey, it's of strategic importance for running cross-country in an east/west direction.

Broadford
Waterside.

SHALFORD LADY

Almost immediately you pass through the embankments of a disused railway link between the Redhill line and the former Horsham to Guildford line. The latter crosses the towpath further up and this loop has been acquired by the National Trust. It is planned to open it up as a footpath with a footbridge over the canal.

The Horsham line was very scenic but unprofitable by the time of the famous Beeching Plan for the railways. Thus it closed on June 12th 1965, just short of its centenary for it had opened on October 2nd 1865. Within two years it was putting the Wey Arun Junction Canal out of business and the Act for closing it was passed by Parliament.

Soon the cottages on the waterfront at Broadford come into view. For long this was heralded by the tall brick chimney of the factory of Vulcanised Fibre Ltd which came here in 1929. Then in 1983 the National Trust was able to reorganise the land use and the ugly old factory was swept away and replaced by the more distinctive modern building. The developers undertook to maintain an attractive river frontage and the National Trust undertook improvements to their own.

Broadford takes its name from the ford that crossed here until a bridge was built in 1793. The bridge was much needed once the river was made navigable. The bargees wanted deeper water than pleased the users of the ford and so, inevitably, disputes arose.

When the next straight stretch begins to turn Stonebridge Wharf is on the far bank. Its remote siting out in the farmland was chosen deliberately for here was loaded the dangerous cargo of gunpowder barrels. For hundreds of years, until 1920 there a gunpowder works of national importance at nearby Chilworth. There's still a lot to see at the site but at Stonebridge the red warning flags no longer fly and the only reminder of those days is the wooden granary shown above. It's the only survivor of two which stood by the wharf, not as granaries but as temporary stores for the gunpowder. Barges taking such a cargo also flew a red flag and had a red line painted round them. This should not be confused with the red livery line on the Stevens' barge at Dapdune Wharf.

84

Beside Stonebridge Wharf you can look into the Guen's Mouth — the name given to the entrance of the Wey Arun Junction Canal — sketched above. It stretches as far as you can see and then becomes disused and overgrown and, in places, lost altogether.

The Act of Parliament for its construction was passed in 1813 and it opened in 1816. It linked the Wey and Arun rivers so there was a waterway link between London and the south coast without going round by sea. Wars with France made that seem a sound proposition.

It was never a great success because the highest point is obviously between the two rivers so water drained out each end. There was a drop of 48 feet to the Wey and 122 feet to the Arun.

Within fifty years the new railways were proving to be faster, more efficient and more popular. They were a decisive factor in the decision to close the canal in 1871.

Next you'll come to the railway footpath and then on to Unstead Lock.

Wild Pansies.

85

UNSTEAD LOCK
TO
CATTESHALL LOCK

Map 186: 992460 to 980445

The walk up to Unstead Lock is beside a channel that was once a mill race but the corn mill, built in 1826, has been replaced by the factory. Water for the mill was drawn off a little upstream and generated the power through the fall in levels at the lock. A sluice in the bank opposite could be operated by the miller to release water to the river beyond and so help control his power.

An 1899 Sales Catalogue in Guildford Museum gives an idea of the mill by listing its machinery :-

    6 pairs of stones
    6 pairs of reduction rolls
    7 pairs of granulation rolls
    Armfield's Patent Centrifugal
        Sifter
    2 smutters for wheat cleaning
    Smith's Patent Centrifugal
        Dressing Machine
    4 other dressing machines
    2 purifiers
    "Koh-I-Noor" Sifter
    2 separating reels
    Large double centrifugal
        dressing machine
    Double rotatary plansifter
    Wheat washing tackle
    2 bran sifters
    4 Van Gilder's Separators
    Oat crusher
    Large chaff cutter
    6 sets of hoisting tackle
    Powerful beam engine
    2 large iron-framed water
        wheels.

More than you imagined ?

Apart from the mill-race the historic past does not draw attention to itself along here. Instead, walkers can enjoy the simple pleasures of the rural landscape, with the addition of low wooded hills.

It is perhaps the richest stretch for the variety of wild flowers, making a June/July walk very memorable. Also, there seem to be many of the dark blue damsel flies, Agrion splendens, with dark blotched wings.

The scene on the left may change little as 50 acres of this riverside land were bought by the National Trust. So was the field on the right after Unstead Bridge and with it came a second World War pillbox.

In the gardens: Pheasant's Eye Narcissi

Top: Fledgling Blackbirds.

From Unstead lock the towpath follows the straight cut of the Godalming Navigation as far as Unstead Sluices. These keep back water to fill the cut and release the surplus to flow off as the river meandering along beside. Further land, on the right, is also safeguarded in the ownership of the National Trust to ward off encroachment by developers. The value of that is soon realised as houses and gardens begin to border the towpath. Fortunately it is still very attractive through here. The trees and flowers of the gardens increase the range of plants to enjoy and attract extra species of birds to look out for.

white-lipped snail. Eats grass in the hedgerows and lettuces in the gardens.

Caterpillar of Lacanobia oleracea, known to naturalists as the Bright-line Brown-eye Moth and to gardeners as the Tomato Moth. It feeds on a variety of plants other than the tomato and is common in gardens.

About halfway along this stretch of housing is the Manor Inn which is thought to have once been the house of George Marshall. He had an invested interest in the Godalming Navigation for not only did he use it for his local timber business but he had also bought a lot of shares in it. In his day, shares were known as "assignments".

Also look out for the backs of the Wyatt Almshouses, especially as the great double chimneys make the back more distinctive than the front. They were paid for by Richard Wyatt of Hall Place, Shackleford and a citizen of London where he was a Freeman of the Worshipful Company of Carpenters. He died in 1619 (buried at Isleworth) and his almshouses were ready in 1622. Entrance for visitors off A3100, the Guildford to Godalming road.

Spot next a chapel of 1789 built for the Unitarians who were first mentioned in Godalming in 1699. That makes them the second oldest non-conformist group, after the Quakers, in this locality. Their chapel and garden can also be visited, from the main road side.

"Japonica"

CATTERSHALL LOCK
TO
GODALMING WHARF

Map 186 : 980445 to 975440

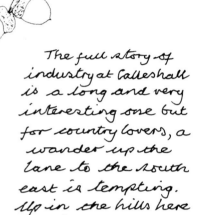

Woodpigeon

After little Trowers Bridge (1789), making smart reflections in the water, the nearness of Cattershall Lock is heralded by the Farncombe Boathouse and all the people it attracts.

The house was built about 1908 on a slip of land between river and navigation, leaving us to wonder why the two were not joined at the lock.

Cattershall, through the 1980s has been the scene of new development but there are still the older factory buildings to add their own level of interest.

Chief among these is Cattershall Mill which became an engineering works. Here the industrial archaeologists found that the turbine installed in 1869 was a rare Fourneyron example.

It was invented in France in the 1820s and was the first successful design. This particular one is believed to be the largest ever made and the oldest to survive so it has the rare distinction (like the Guildford Treadwheel Crane) of being scheduled as an ancient monument. For restoration purposes it has been removed to Westbrook Mills upstream. Its eventual home has not been decided yet (1989).

The full story of industry at Cattershall is a long and very interesting one but for country lovers, a wander up the lane to the south east is tempting. Up in the hills here was built the old manor. Henry I granted it to Dyrus Purcell. His son, Geoffrey, was the King's Usher of the Chamber, responsible for the linen and the launderesses. Perhaps it was too much for him — he retreated to the famous Abbey at Reading to be a monk. He gave Cattershall to the Abbey.

Further up in the hills is Munstead, where Gertrude Jekyll lived and worked. Her famous strain of 'Munstead' primroses were developed from a plant she spotted in a garden in Farncombe about 1873. Among the many plants she developed locally was a pure blue form of Pulmonaria (left) still sold as 'Munstead Blue'. Of the many local buildings and scenes in her writings, Munstead Farm at Cattershall is still recognisable.

After the buildings of Catteshall it's back to the meadows again; the usual contrast but no less welcome for that although this is the last time. Godalming Wharf lies ahead.

The open fields are called the Lammas Lands from the days of communal farming when the first corn of the harvest was baked into a special loaf for consecrating at Mass — Loaf Mass or Lammas. Traditionally this was on 1st August. The farming here was organised by the courts of Catteshall Manor.

In 1981 flocks of geese strutted through the grass to be sketched quickly (above) as such 'Victorian' subjects do not occur often.

Time has been fairly easy on Godalming, allowing the common fields to survive next to town centre. Time has not, however, left us anything at the wharf.

Barge kettle that won't rock off the stove.

Even before being given to the National Trust, land at the wharf had been developed for different purposes. Thus the Trust found themselves owners of their only filling station, only bus station etc.

In the 1980s opportunities arose to make more sense of the situation so the Trust got together with Waverley Borough Council. Ownerships were changed and with the money raised the Trust was able to improve its river-frontage and work on other sites.

That then is some of the interest along the towpath but before going home to put the kettle on try a boat trip......

GODALMING WHARF

HORSE DRAWN NARROWBOAT TRIPS

No exploration of the Navigations is complete without a trip in a horse drawn boat as per the days of old. This was becoming a scarce sight by late Victorian times. In 1884 Sir Charles Dilke observed, "The towing of small boats is now almost exclusively by people: there are very boats towed by horses. For every boat towed by a horse there are at least two or three hundred towed by people; that is the new custom."

From Godalming Wharf you can journey for two hours on the "Iona" which began her life in 1935 as the "Bellerophon". She is a star class narrowboat built at Woolwich by Harland and Wolff for the Grand Union Canal Carrying Company.

For her early life the boat carried bulk cargoes such as coal to London and returned with wheat, steel billets and lime juice. In 1964 she was converted for carrying passengers on the Shropshire Union Canal.

"Baccarat"

In 1984 "Iona" was brought south to Godalming. She is 70 feet long and 7 feet wide which is the maximum size possible on the Midland canals.

Mrs Jenny Roberts now employs "Iona" to carry up to 48 persons, whether on special trips for schools and private groups or as a regular pleasure for summer visitors who've booked a place or arrive at the wharf hoping for one.

For current details and bookings ring 04868 – 4938 or
     04868 – 25397   (the wharf no.)

My thanks to Jenny Roberts and her team for allowing me to feature their enterprise and publish the illustrations.

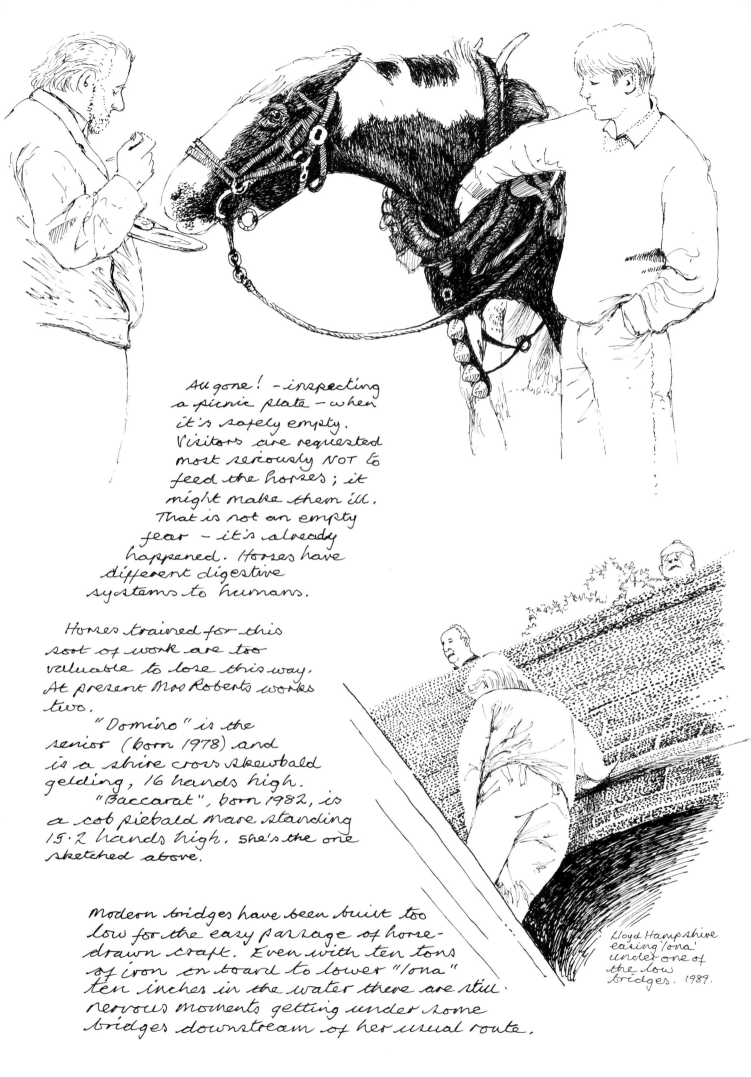

All gone! – inspecting
a picnic plate – when
it's safely empty.
Visitors are requested
most seriously NOT to
feed the horses; it
might make them ill.
That is not an empty
fear – it's already
happened. Horses have
different digestive
systems to humans.

Horses trained for this
sort of work are too
valuable to lose this way.
At present Mrs Roberts works
two.
   "Domino" is the
senior (born 1978) and
is a shire cross skewbald
gelding, 16 hands high.
   "Baccarat", born 1982, is
a cob piebald mare standing
15·2 hands high. She's the one
sketched above.

Modern bridges have been built too
low for the easy passage of horse-
drawn craft. Even with ten tons
of iron on board to lower "Iona"
ten inches in the water there are still
nervous moments getting under some
bridges downstream of her usual route.

Lloyd Hampshire
easing 'Iona'
under one of
the low
bridges. 1989.

92

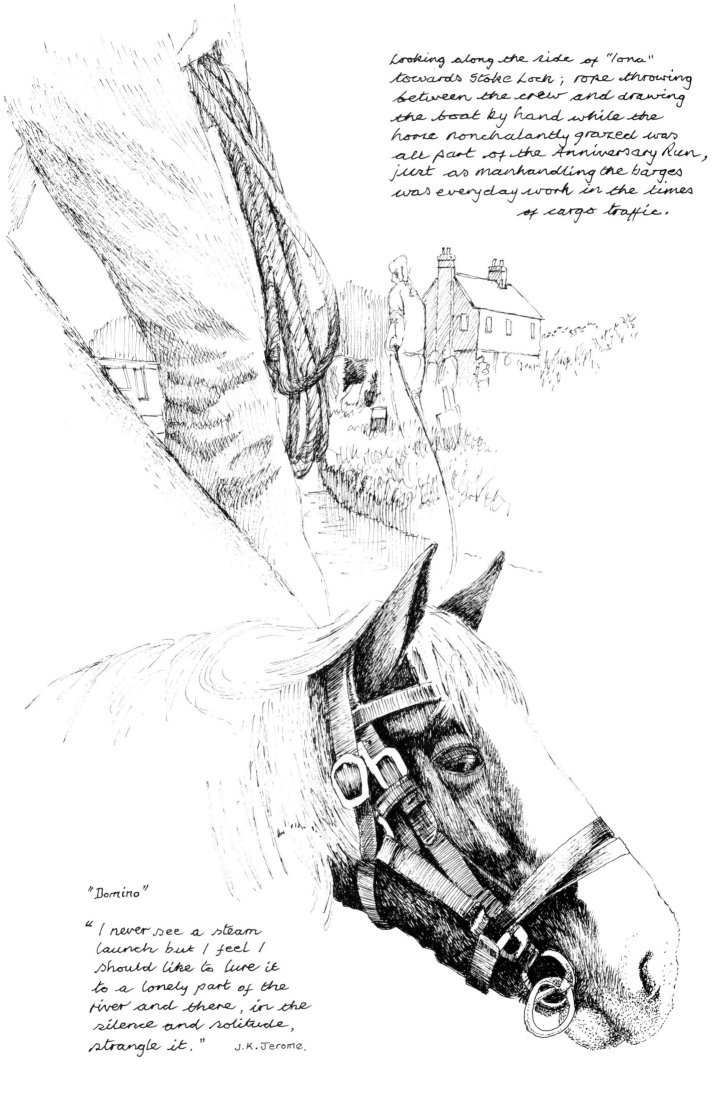

Looking along the side of "Iona" towards Stoke Lock; rope throwing between the crew and drawing the boat by hand while the horse nonchalantly grazed was all part of the Anniversary Run, just as manhandling the barges was everyday work in the times of cargo traffic.

"Domino"

" I never see a steam
launch but I feel I
should like to lure it
to a lonely part of the
river and there, in the
silence and solitude,
strangle it. "
                    J.K.Jerome.

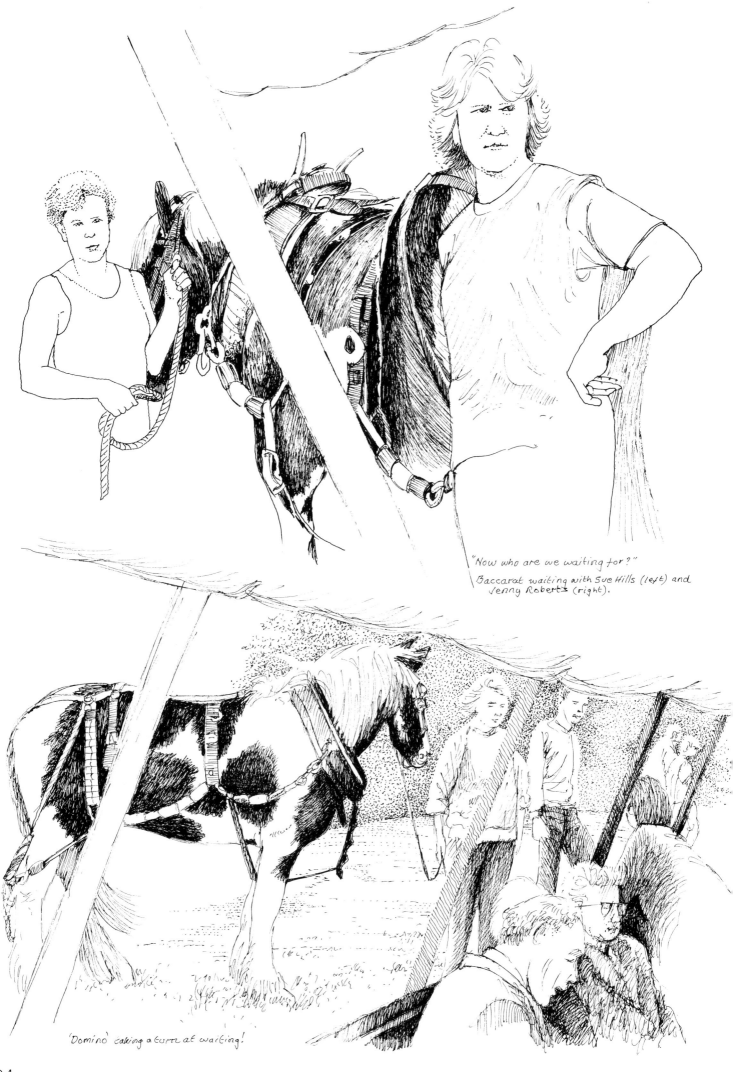

"Now who are we waiting for?"
Baccarat waiting with Sue Hills (left) and
Jenny Roberts (right).

'Domino' taking a turn at waiting!

There is much more to see and enjoy along the Wey Navigation than has been possible to squeeze into these pages.

Of course it is all very different now from when the man on the left, Mr. Steve White, spent his working life as a bargee on the river, as did his father and grandfather before him. Even the London Docks which he knew so well have now gone. How Mr. White's eyes shone when he recalled them: strange ships and costumes, names and languages, cargoes and smells. All the world came to London and the Wey Navigation brought a bit of it into the heart of Surrey.

"Iona" (left) and "Lynx" (right) at Millmead, 10·9·1989.

Mr. White's memories were published in 1985 as "Captain White's River Life."

95

ACKNOWLEDGEMENTS

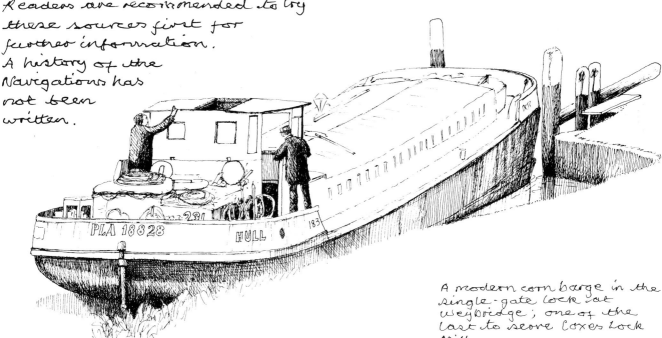

In addition to all the local historians, museum curators and officers of the National Trust who helped me create the first Towpath Book I should now like to thank all those who have made this second version possible.

Few of them are known to me by name! They've been members of audiences who have stood up at the end of one of my talks and said, "Did you know that....." and there was another piece of the story to go away and check and add to the files.

One man whom I can thank by name is Mr. Bob Nicholls who succeeded Mr. Ratcliffe as Manager of the Wey Navigation and who always found time in his hectic day to help. Thanks also to all the other members of the team who maintain the Navigation and have been equally generous with their time whenever asked.

Thanks also to Prof. Alan Crocker and his wife for sharing their knowledge of the industrial archaeology, from gunpowder to turbines, and, to Mrs. J. Roberts and her team for not only sharing information but for so generously allowing me to publish the sketches of them at work.

Finally, I am very thankful for the time and skill given by the workforce at Unwin Brothers Ltd when it came to converting my manuscript into book form.

SOURCES

Oral information has been checked wherever possible with the officers of the National Trust, the Local Studies Library at Guildford and with the staff and records of the district museums at Godalming, Guildford and Weybridge. Readers are recommended to try these sources first for further information. A history of the Navigations has not been written.

TEACHERS

For help with local studies, talks to schools and the use of film slides that are available, teachers are invited to write to the publisher's address.

A modern corn barge in the single-gate lock at Weybridge; one of the last to serve Coxes Lock Mill.